BEST CANADIAN POETRY 2025

AISLINN HUNTER, GUEST EDITOR
ANITA LAHEY, SERIES EDITOR

BIBLIOASIS
WINDSOR, ONTARIO

FIRST EDITION
ISBN 978-1-77196-632-0 (Trade Paper)
ISBN 978-1-77196-633-7 (eBook)

Guest-edited by Aislinn Hunter
Series edited by Anita Lahey
Editorial assistant: Ashley Van Elswyk
Copyedited and typeset by Vanessa Stauffer
Series designed by Ingrid Paulson

Published with the generous assistance of the Canada Council for the Arts, which last year invested $153 million to bring the arts to Canadians throughout the country, and the financial support of the Government of Canada. Biblioasis also acknowledges the support of the Ontario Arts Council (OAC), an agency of the Government of Ontario, which last year funded 1,709 individual artists and 1,078 organizations in 204 communities across Ontario, for a total of $52.1 million, and the contribution of the Government of Ontario through the Ontario Book Publishing Tax Credit and Ontario Creates.

PRINTED AND BOUND IN CANADA

CONTENTS

Foreword 11
Introduction 17

Billy-Ray Belcourt   *According to the CBC,*
Indigenous Peoples Are
Demonstrably More Vulnerable
to Illness and Disease, Live 15
Years Less Than Other
Canadians 25

Miranda Pearson   *Bridestones* 27

Susan Gillis   *Come In, Come In* 29

George Amabile   *Coming of age on my 84th*
birthday 31

Owen Torrey   *CV* 33

Lorna Crozier   *December's End* 35

Michael Trussler   *~~Decoy~~* 36

Catherine Owen   *Fall* 37

Shannon Quinn   *Feral* 38

Hollie Adams   *Five Days a Week* 39

Catherine St. Denis   *Five Years After Joe*
                          Overdosed on Fentanyl 42

Karen Solie   *Flashlight* 45

Erin Bedford   *For my dad who never*
                   read my poems but died with
                   a well-thumbed copy of
                   Watership Down 47

Emily Cann   *The Fox* 49

Anne Carson   *Funny You Should Ask* 51

Anne Simpson   *The Golden Boat* 54

Carolyn Smart   *Grip* 57

Y. S. Lee   *He/him* 58

Molly Cross-Blanchard   *Here's the thing* 59

Molly Peacock   *Honey Crisp* 61

Pauline Peters   *Housebreaking* 63

Elisabeth Blair   *a hunt's surviving duck* 64

D. A. Lockhart   *Hussain Recites Ginsberg
While Driving Down Kedzie* 65

Kim June Johnson   *I Don't Know What to Do about
the World* 67

Amanda Proctor   *I found a place where time
stands still* 68

Domenica Martinello   *Infinity Mirror* 70

Catherine Graham   *Last Shadow* 72

Robert Bringhurst   *Life Poem* 74

Alison Braid-Fernandez   *Light Upon the Body* 79

Evelyn Lau   *Mindful* 80

Henry Heavyshield   *My Brother,* Om'ahkokata
(gopher) 82

Rob Winger   *Near Dark Park* 87

Evelyna Ekoko-Kay   *on my shoulders* 89

Jaeyun Yoo   *Orchids* 92

Alexander Hollenberg   *origin story, with crow* 93

Bertrand Bickersteth   *A Poem about Blackboy's Horse* 95

Fareh Malik   *Praise Us, for We Are Dead* 97

Armand Garnet Ruffo   *Resting II* 99

Kayla Czaga   *Safe Despair* 101

Cassidy McFadzean   *Storm King* 105

Erín Moure   *The Straying of All Translation: A Phrase Archive* 106

Eve Joseph   *superpowers* 107

Sue Goyette   *surprise: an armoire (in a sunny spot, I'm hoping)* 108

David Martin   *Tinnitus* 111

Gerald Hill   *To Celebrate Waves Right to Left in a Shirt-Rippling Wind, Tavira, Portugal* 112

Tolu Oloruntoba   *"Understand me, love me, answer me": 77 Questions from Anne Szumigalski* 113

Carmelita McGrath   *Visit, July 25, 2020* 118

Kate Genevieve   *Wheels on the Bus Go* 121

Ronna Bloom   *Where I've Been* 122

Sara Truuvert   *You Grew an Orange* 123

Notes 125
Contributors' Commentary
  and Biographies 131
Notable Poems 163
Magazines Consulted 167
Index to Poets 173
Acknowledgements 175
Editors' Biographies 181

FOREWORD

How to Let Poems Be

The first poem in this, the sixteenth annual edition of *Best Canadian Poetry*, will usher you into the flat aching heart of a Canadian prairie. Don't roll your eyes. This is no naive CanLit pastoral. By the time you step out onto the plains, you'll have felt the breeze from the door of death swinging open, then swirled in an eddy of bewilderment and loss. And now, a "better myth": a woman who'll "give birth to two boys at once," and then, with nothing but her gaze (powered, you can feel it, by love), make them beautiful, and in that beauty, capable of inventing, again and again, their own methods of survival.

Paraphrasing poetry is problematic. My description of this poem is way too lovely. In fact, the poem is cinematic, electric, a full set of lungs poised to unleash a summer storm. The title chosen by its author, Billy-Ray Belcourt, places it first in the book alphabetically. It's also audacious, taking up four full lines: "According to the CBC, Indigenous Peoples Are Demonstrably More Vulnerable to Illness and Disease, Live 15 Years Less Than Other Canadians." It's literally a piece of a reportage.

It's the sort of title—and this is no knock on the poem—that a person interviewing a poet on the radio would love. Writers (for that matter, artists of all stripes) are forever being asked what their work is "about," what they "want people to take" from their work. My dismay at the frequency of such questions is overridden only by my surprise at how readily so many authors will answer them, as if there can be an answer to such a query, or should be.

Whatever gets a poem going, whether idea, query, fact, experience, memory, or emotion—more likely some combination—will lead the poet along, and rightly inform their use of language and form. But then what? Through attention, focus, and revision; through an intent form of listening and concentration; through a practiced blend of composing-and-shaping, instinctive yet considered, for which poets strive; something emerges, ideally something that the poet was both aiming for and couldn't have predicted, or come anywhere near articulating outside of the poem.

In asserting that we can feel the love in Belcourt's poem, I don't mean as an abstraction. I mean that it burbles and sputters in the underwater heaven evoked by the speaker's kokum. That it lies splayed along the em-dash that reaches out from Belcourt's "unclaimable joy." I mean especially that it rears as the mother looks at her sons, and that it shadows the distant, lumbering "blurry beast" of our country "roaming too close to the horizon / to be anything but imaginary." Here resides a furious indictment of Canada, a fury rooted in love of the land (and people) it has claimed. The love in the poem claims its own space, right alongside the statistic cited in the title; it's doing its damnedest to even the odds. And when we read the poem, we activate and release it.

The effect can be unsettling. After reading a strong, sound poem like Belcourt's, I feel thrown. I'm like a jittery bee that a tulip has just spat out, dazed from my roll in a sticky, bottomless bed of pollen. Wow. What happened back there? Was that for real? The poem can't explain it; it's no more articulate than the tulip or the bee, or, for that matter, the pollen.

By now, as we piece together the final components of this anthology, I've read the poems within many times. Each reading of each poem offers a fresh immersion, a new experience coloured by the moment of our meeting: the time of day; the weather; the room I'm in (as distinct from the world of the poem); my mood; the images, word-sounds, and correspondences that strike me harder or differently than last time I visited this place. Increasingly, as I return to them, I'm struck by matters that speak not just to the poems themselves, but to questions of poetry: what we expect from it, what happens when we encounter it, where it comes from, and, finally, what it actually is. In his essay "Poetry and Thinking," collected in his book *The Tree of Meaning: Thirteen Talks*, Robert Bringhurst (whose "Life Poem" appears in this volume) compares poetry to science, describing it as "a way of finding out—by trying to state clearly and perceptively—what is going on." As it does for scientists, Bringhurst explains, the work of a poet lies in "learning *how* to think, not deciding *what* to believe."

My account of my experience with "According to the CBC ..." illustrates how, fundamentally, poems are not *about* things, first promising and then delivering the goods. To read a fully realized poem is to have a visceral encounter with the right words in the right order, which have caught hold of some elemental aspect of our reality. Reading such verse is like plunging into the pollen-caked flower, so what about the mess. I've got poem all over me now: I've got something intoxicating, something weirdly familiar and strange, something necessary for the very survival of my species, to ferry home.

*

Aislinn Hunter, the guest editor of *Best Canadian Poetry 2025*, selected the poem I kept company with above, as well as the forty-nine others collected here—each its own cache of wildness—from dozens of editions of print and online journals that published poems by Canadian authors in 2023. The goal? To offer a series of glimpses that morph into a fairly coherent overview of the current state of poetry in Canada: who is writing, and what, and how? And from all that compulsive versifying—to write poems is irresistible to those who engage in the practice, believe me—which are the poems we wish to bring together here, in hopes that we don't lose sight of them as the next year's avalanche of magazines and poems thunders our way? This anthology serves as a pause, an annual reckoning for anyone who reads, write, studies, cares about or is curious about contemporary Canadian poetry.

Like all of BCP's guest editors going back to our first edition in 2008, Hunter read avidly and widely. She came out on the other side of a year spent with contemporary poets to make this declaration, which appears in her moving and revelatory introductory essay in these pages: "I believe that poems behave like living things."

It's an assertion that brings to mind fanged, growling books about fantastical beasts, kept safely shut with sturdy clasps. It also brings to mind the tenor of her own work as a novelist, essayist and poet. In her ambitious, affecting novels, such as *The World Before Us* and *The Certainties*; in her inventive, illuminating book of essays, *Peepshow With Views of the Interior: Paratexts* (comprised wholly of front and back matter); and in her three graceful, big-hearted volumes of poetry, Hunter ranges through philosophy, mythology, and the cosmos; pandemics and wars; the beguiling resonance of *things* (her scholarly specialty), from boots to buttons to bones; her own raw, close-up, unmediated grief. Her probing is made gentle by its being palpably lit and warm, generously tactile and sensory. Her admissions of plain, simple wonder pop up like benches in dappled shade, gifts she holds out to her readers.

Hunter's awe is not wide-eyed but brought on, like the love in Belcourt's poem, through the sheer force of her peering, by her tacit belief that the keen attention she brings—the same regard brought to each of the fifty poems in this book, and to each of those named as Notable Poems—is an honest offering, a reaching out. In "Northwestern Salamander Eggs Preserved in a Jar," from her newest poetry collection, *Linger, Still*—an eloquent and uplifting confrontation with the human condition—she finds "a hundred slow curtsies / in filmy skirts" at which she looks so intently that, like Alice, she falls right through the glass:

How clear it is here
in the filigreed cloud of this
ancient bedding,
to see that being born is the rarity—
to see how the odds are stacked
against navigation—
to marvel at the possibility
of arrival, at how anything
becomes anything
at all.

How *do* things *become*? One way is by being seen and heard. In the essay that follows, Hunter advocates reading poems aloud. I heartily second this. Better still, read poems in company. Share them with others who also like to sidle up to the music of the line. I don't propose teasing them apart with wary eyes peeled for subterfuge. True poets are not trying to show you up—rather, to invite you along. Their poems are small offerings, meant (even when radiating anguish, confusion, or rage) to be enjoyed: the roll of their sounds over your tongue; how they rise and fall, undulate and spin; their hollers and whispers and asides; their bursts of contempt and soft settlings into forgiveness; their weird leaps; their textures and shapes; their wafts of memory and scent.

"Poetry is what I start to hear when I concede the world's ability to manage and to understand itself," Bringhurst writes. "It is the language of the world: something humans overhear if they are willing to pay attention, and something that the world will teach us to speak, if we allow the world to do so."

That is the thing about poetry: we don't create it by writing it or by reading it. It's already there. I should say, it's here. Available and willing, should we come looking.

Anita Lahey
unceded Algonquin, Anishinabek
territory / Ottawa
April 2024

INTRODUCTION

Why Poetry

When my husband was in the late stages of his terminal illness, he asked me to read him poetry. He didn't ask for short stories, or essays, or news articles, or the first crisp pages of a novel, with its unfolding narrative weight. The request was unexpected. Despite his five (almost five and a half) decades on this earth, he'd never been much of a reader, though he was incredibly knowledgeable about the world, often serving as my first editor, catching errors or incongruities in my poetry or prose, the wrong slip of a word. And so, without much thought as to why poetry, most evenings I obliged him: ferrying a few collections from my study to the living room where he lay on a rented hospital bed, largely paralyzed from both his brain tumour and the muscle-weakening trudge of a year and a half on medications aimed at keeping him alive. From an old loveseat, under faerie lights, our three dogs sleeping around us, I'd read a poem or two from each book, never dwelling too long on one poet in case the poems I'd selected didn't speak to him in the way he hoped, in that moment, to be spoken to. I suppose, in a strange way, I was curating an anthology for him. What strikes me now, about the poems I chose to read to him in late 2018, is how steeped they were in tenderness and knowing.

There was one poet's knowing of his own impending death, there was another poet's Buddhist knowing of the transient, and poem after poem about the knowing of love—what it means to try at that beautiful and hopeful thing, whether that light is directed at the self, or another, or the world. I've thought a lot about "why poetry" this past year. Why it is, to my mind, the most powerful and instantaneous of the arts. The feeling I get from encountering a good poem is like turning around on a busy street only to discover I've nearly collided with a stranger: the two of us suddenly close in an unexpected and vivifying way. I admire the visual arts—galleries are one of my life's great pleasures—but in apprehending an artwork there still seems to be a kind of mediating distance that is greater than the intimacy felt when reading a poem. Poetry's cousin, music, is immediate in its own way, but often the maker of the music seems distant—on the other side of the swelling strings and swirling oboes and the musicians playing the composer's notes. In poetry you have your hand on someone else's heartbeat.

In his wonderful book *Art Matters,* cultural history scholar Peter de Bolla investigates the intense somatic responses we can have when engaging with art. In an essay that focusses on literature, he describes how the act of reading is intertwined with the making of meaning, noting that—compared to other creative activities that involve listening and looking—reading is deeply and intensely immediate: "[T]he reading and the response are interactive; that is, one develops in the shadow and in step with the other." In "Phenomenology of Reading," the philosopher Georges Poulet posits something similar when he describes the cohabitation that occurs between the reader and the written material. He writes, "The work lives its own life within me; in a certain sense, it thinks itself, and it even gives itself a meaning within me." He identifies a consciousness within the work that is active, potent. I felt this frequently in my year of reading: aware that I was having conversations *with* the poems; that the poets were offering their services as correspondents, interlocutors, field reporters, guides.

I believe that poems behave like living things. They open and close, they shift and grow. Poetry's essential elements move into us—letter and word shapes swimming past retinal neurons and along phonological and lexical routes, eventually meeting neurons and synapses that light up the forest / the temple / the mess hall of our brains. Language—poetry's essence—changes our physiology, which is to say that a poem's doing *to us* is as real as rain on skin. Of course, the power of the art we're meeting matters, as does the state of alertness we're in.

*

There were two quotes framed beside our bed in the year and three-quarters between my husband Glenn's terminal diagnosis and his death. The first was the Arabic proverb: "When danger approaches, sing to it." The second was this excerpt from a poem by Robert Hass:

> We asked the captain what course
> of action he proposed to take toward
> a beast so large, terrifying, and
> unpredictable. He hesitated to
> answer, and then said judiciously:
> "I think I shall praise it."

As a consolatory fellow traveller, poetry does something that other forms of writing do less expediently. With breathtaking compression and density, poetry praises the insoluble and the difficult. It says *Here's this event that I've lived,* or *Here's this grief, this want, this wildness, this lie I'm living but can't sustain, here's this beautiful moment—its fulfillment tinged by the blue dusk of its inevitable going ... Here's me looking at it so intently its form comes into sharp relief. Here's me risking what it means to feel it into language.*

As I read through this year's excellent crop of literary journals and online magazines my worldview expanded. I stood behind thousands of others, peering through their viewfinders at the cities, towns, landscapes, and rooms they inhabited. I took a rideshare with one poet, sat on a rooftop deck with another, soaked seeds with a third, visited a public pond, went for surgery, searched a gully, watched stars collapse, studied a crow. The most impactful poems I read were sites of feeling—which is to say sites of inquiry, resistance, resilience, regret, provocation, play, grief, desire, glee ... The poems I dog-eared felt confident and necessary. They were speaking about where we are now. Reviewing the final one hundred and fifty or so poems felt like moving through a house that existed in some kind of Borgesian story: every window offering a different vista, every return to that view affected by the day's changing weather—which is to say my own shifting moods; my happiness or haste; the news. Sometimes, from the safety of this dreamed-up house and my own bright study, I imagined other houses in other countries, some twin editor in their windowed rooms. What would an anthology of best Ukrainian poetry look like in these times, or a collection from Angola, or Gaza?

Subjects that appeared frequently in the poetry zeitgeist this year included grief (personal and planetary), identity, ancestry and ancestors, violence and resilience, the body, past reckonings, poverty, and language. There were issues dedicated to ghosts (*Room*), dreams and nightmares (*Vallum*), hauntings (*Prairie Fire*), disability and desirability (*Arc*), IBPOC writing (*Prism*), and Indigenous storytelling (*Ex-Puritan*). There were lots of poems about seeing and re-seeing the landscapes we move in, and poems that sought to evoke some of the animals we share the planet with. These were especially interesting to me.

Writing about animals is common in literature, but the way some poets *write* animals—especially around point of view—is changing. The philosopher Josephine Donovan, in *Animals, Mind, and Matter*, describes this animal-forward perspective as an ethic of care. She reminds us that "animals can and do communicate to humans about how they wish to be treated and how they wish—and need—to live." And that "[a]pplying care/standpoint theory to animal ethics means listening therefore to the 'voice' of animals, hearing their standpoint vis-á-vis a system that oppresses them." Considerations of an animal's standpoint were braided into a number of the poems that I read this year, and in some that appear in this anthology. In 2021, the Innu First Nation's Mutehekau Shipu (Magpie River) was granted legal personhood in Canada—our first river to be granted this status. The Nonhuman Rights Project (operating internationally) has been working on a case-by-case basis to give animals the legal status of persons as well. The case is compelling and just. I see this advocacy and these shifts reflected in films, in literature, in social discourse, and in this year's poems. In Canada, I attribute some of this shift, at least in settler cultures, to the foregrounding of Indigenous ways of knowing, and of relating to animals and the earth.

It's also possible that in times of peril, poetry demands more dynamic ways of seeing. As I started reading my first journals this year, scientists announced that one million species were on the brink of extinction. By the time I read my last journal, wildfires across this country had torched a staggering—and record-setting—16.5 million hectares of land. This notice of mass extinction, these blazing red flags, are prompting heightened forms of attention to the natural world and its inhabitants. In his thought-provoking (and playful) Anne Szumigalski lecture, published in *Prairie Fire*, Tolu Oloruntoba (whose Szumigalski cento appears in this anthology) notes that, "when poetry is deployed (written, read, or recited) in settings of existential anxiety, although poetry does not replace actual therapy, it can be therapeutic." To read so many poets wrestling with the cost of human expansion over the planet *was* comforting, as if an urgent town meeting had been called.

*

As a year's worth of literary magazines started to take over a whole corner of my study (I had to move one of the dogs' beds; she did not approve!) I developed a shambolic theory: the notion that the most impactful poems often felt *true* or *perfect,* and sometimes—excitingly—both. The *true* poems had the feeling of a necessary utterance, of strong praxis ("praxis" in poetry, for me, is what Dante called "a movement of spirit"). The *perfect* poems had all the right words in the right order and a register of surprise (fresh images or startling language; unexpected turns). The poems that embodied both these attributes seemed to demand my attention through a suasive voice that felt thoroughly present and awake. And so, my year of reading was also a kind of dialogue with the poems: how did that one win me over? How did this one bring me into its centre? The poets whose poems I returned to were doing sly work, sounding both artful and unrehearsed.

Time with poetry is rarely wasted. Part of what I appreciated about the poems I selected is that none of them made me wait in line, none of them asked me to tap or swipe, or tried to sell me a condo, or evict me, or pressure me into extra insurance. None of them promised me eternal happiness in a jar. The poetry I read this year spoke to salient things. Though, thankfully, poetry also likes to have a good laugh. Throughout my year of reading, I felt tremendous gratitude for the poets, the poems, and for the literary magazine editors and first readers who facilitate these conversations. I enjoyed reading the poems aloud to myself, and sometimes, in the late stages of my selections, together with BCP's series editor, Anita Lahey, from our book-filled studies three time zones apart. Hearing a poem read aloud is a wonderful thing. I encourage you to try reading some of these out loud to yourself, or to a friend. I've used editions of *Best Canadian Poetry* as first-year creative writing textbooks for years. In my classes, we read poems out loud. Hearing the same poem vocalized by apprentice writers of different ages and disparate backgrounds—with their sometimes confident, sometimes wondering voices—brings each poem to light in a new hue.

So, again, why poetry? In Nigerian writer Ben Okri's essay on writing and the climate crisis, he calls for an existential creativity "wherein nothing should be wasted." He says: "I must write now as if these are the last things I will write, that any of us will write.

If you knew you were at the last days of the human story, what would you write? How would you write? What would your aesthetics be? Would you use more words than necessary? What form would poetry truly take?" Here he names poetry, calling for it in this dusking hour the same way my husband did, because it is a way of singing towards the danger.

My friend, the late writer Steve Heighton, once wrote: "Writers, like others, live in hope, only more so … Hope means leaning into the future, anticipating a maybe instead of living an is." In my year of reading, I rode a ferry with one poet, fell off a horse with another, I went ice-skating, visited New York, picked up a flashlight, crossed a field as a gopher, was watched by Life, stood witness over graves, was moored under a moon, and drove around in a car with Death and Emily Dickinson. I listened to one poet ask how to love the world and then stood with another as a broken bowl repaired itself. There were tremors of hope everywhere. Poetry, after all, is a form of exalted saying. And this, I think, is the other part of why poetry. Because poems, through their prismatic attention and language-care, lift life a little bit higher. And with that, we are sometimes lifted too.

Aislinn Hunter
from the unceded and territorial lands of the Musqueam,
Squamish and Tsleil-Waututh peoples
April 2024

Billy-Ray Belcourt

ACCORDING TO THE CBC, INDIGENOUS PEOPLES ARE DEMONSTRABLY MORE VULNERABLE TO ILLNESS AND DISEASE, LIVE 15 YEARS LESS THAN OTHER CANADIANS

In my country,
death is a door
that swings open.
Onto all the trees
in the neighbourhood
I wrote: UP CLOSE AN NDN
IS A DEMONSTRABLE IMPOSSIBILITY.
When I lived in the UK,
no one knew what I was.
It was another kind of unfreedom,
because my suffering was still Indigenous.
When I told my kokum I was homesick,
she said: *If heaven is a place, my dear,*
I'm afraid it's already underwater.
I don't yet know how to mourn
the loss of all those years
before I've lost them,
all that unclaimable joy—
but enough about that cruel math.

Here's a better myth:
Somewhere in the prairies,
a woman gives birth to two boys at once.
They are both beautiful,
but only when she is looking at them.
For decades, Canada is a blurry beast
roaming too close to the horizon
to be anything but imaginary.
Every day they don't die
isn't of statistical importance.
And so, every day they wake up
they invent another way to be
unconquerable.

—from *Arc Poetry Magazine*

Miranda Pearson

BRIDESTONES

You do nothing casual here
                    —Ted Hughes

High on the Pennine Moor,
an outcrop of stones—a congregation,

their elephant boulder-memory.
A woman's place, on the edge.

Here are hags, giant frozen waves,
their spy-holes and hollows.

Here are eons, brief Braille of lichen,
and the years of space between us.

A constellation of absences,
forgiveness, the necessary burying of hurts.

Our ageing. Words we don't and
Can't say, gaps weathered into sculpture.

The fine brush stroke
of our hard-earned lightheartedness.

(Toad-rock   table-rock,
                    stack and loaf)

Past rock's shoulder: blue glimpse of fields.
Man's stone walls straight, and well meant.

We have not lived within such walls.
Our hands held in the un-farmed heather.

Millstone grit, wind-worn heads,
bear, walrus. Hollowed cup-marks and basins,

tiny birds that sing full-throated
on their risen thrones.

—from *Grain*

Susan Gillis

COME IN, COME IN

The breeze is cool, the air warm, or is it the reverse?
Leaves fly up, funnelled by wind.

The tree that shimmered a week ago is bare,
Look! How golden, I said,

and didn't look again until today.
The sky, too, is heavy. Nevertheless the nights

are still too warm for the duvet. And a little giddy.
How do I do it? How does anyone.

Something gathers and wants utterance, wants
out of the throat. Not comfort.

Behold: thirty years ago a summer afternoon
on a rooftop deck above Fan Tan Alley.

Someone is desperate for a cigarette.
Another is saying *are you sure,* the kindest thing.

Watching certain shows is like eating a bucket of KFC
and needing to wash afterwards. Sometimes I want

the twentieth century back, but only the good parts,
swarms of birds in evening light, swellings that aren't blights

or cancers but clean tides spilling into granite, forming pools.
Schoenbergian nights, tears leaking from statuary, hands

pulling a windbreaker tight because the breeze is cool, that's all.
The western sky is flocked like 1950s wallpaper, real

paper pasted onto real walls, walls
that surround our equipment and bring the idea of doors

back to us from metaphor where they wait like birthday presents
to be chosen. Can you hear the far wind stirring

the swimming pools, rattling the blue tarps of surface tension?
Come in, come in, they say. *Come on in.*

—from *The Fiddlehead*

George Amabile

COMING OF AGE ON MY 84TH BIRTHDAY

Something I should have learned when I was young
enough to take it seriously explodes, slowly
like a zucchini blossom, announcing
another surprise in the laddered shades of aging.

Forget the calendar with its beaches
and snow-tufted cedars. Think instead
of the way music tends to extend the distance
between now, and now again. Time,

a perplexity of stars and planets, deft
conjectures and a down-to-earth
god, incarnate in one line of a poem
grass … the beautiful uncut hair

of graves, not yet but close enough
to wake up the Buddhist emptiness I
missed in a lifetime of lectures, paper
futures, mainline entertainments …

Something I already know
too many names for changes
like the flame from a sunset lake
in that moment before the last light

fails, and maybe much too late I'm
in love with everything that remains
unsaid, unsayable but suddenly heard
in the sound of rain on a slate roof.

—from *Poetry Pause*

Owen Torrey

CV

Now I'm remembering another
Thing. A job I had. It was down
By the lake. It wasn't the worst.
The hours were long. The cold
Cold. I didn't mind. I was fine
With that. After all what really
Made it worth it was getting
To see what was left after you
Lifted the ice out. When it came
Out it was a cone mostly. Some
Times a cube. Then some days
I saw two trout peering up out
Through the hole I had made.
Four eyes. Looking lost. Get in
Line, I wanted to say. I will say
I'm finding it hard to find things
Easy. To find things good. Things
Like you. Like life. And like you
Said the core delusion is the fact
That what is not happening to us
Is. At night now I hear ice break
On the lake and think when that
Was me. Who's there now? I am
Absent. If anyone is talking to you
Now it's you. Not me. Yes every

Thing goes these days. Even these
Days go. And we just live like that.

—from *The Malahat Review*

Lorna Crozier

DECEMBER'S END

The first night of the Cold Moon.
Rising in the east, it lays its eye on me.
I am barely here, part of me
gone with my dead husband though I'm not
refined enough to know where that is
or what I'm seeing beyond his pale
drug-swollen face. In the garden
the chilled air feathers me
with frost, head to toe, it rimes
my tongue. Even if I knew what to say
I couldn't say it, I am wintered
with woe, I am flensed, my bones
moving to the surface
their startled, cold-moon shine.

—from *Riddle Fence*

Michael Trussler

~~DECOY~~

> *Poetry is an artifact of the world that has ended.*
>   —Michael Robbins, "A Conversation About Trees"

Hard to disagree. An extinct word-ivore. An improvised glass
sutra sodden as Mylar's hybridity but inert. As shape-shifting

as unintended original sin. Therefore nothing, really. Therefore
now becoming a hobby-store-rocket word that stalls mid-air

incandescent

in the simple science of lighting the birthday candle world.
Fancy recitations. Conceits. This excavating the birthday candle

world wearing a life that's too big too small on each of us
renovating ↔ conjuring ↔ summoning ↔ evacuating

nothing, really. A grindhouse   a wavelength   a very difficult
a cannot properly   a mismatched   a dear   gesture   a
                                                        lure

—from *Grain*

Catherine Owen

FALL

The weather says red sun
as a typical apparition.
Waking to a bathe of crimson,
sanguinary, carmine is just another
summer's day,
the sun a mouth announcing the latest
fires: garbage, recklessness, oil, no
source reported but that it's regular,
nothing special about the apocalypse
anymore nor has there ever been with Thor
or Kali or the Cold War or that fabled button
of nuclear brutishness.
Yet the weather is saying more now of less,
fewer species, dwindled forests.
Cut, we say, chop, burn.
And the weather says, catch.

—from *The Fiddlehead*

Shannon Quinn

FERAL

Light starved whispers slid
into our beds   we called them gods
They stayed through the night
while a shadow watched
from our bedroom door as we slept

They showed us a mouse was a leaf was
a piece of skin from the sky   that wind
was nature's resurrection & wasn't that
a bit of unredeemed magic—
a flagrant grace turned wild with wonder

They circled us, singing that the shades
of loneliness & grief had married the shadows
from our childhood & forgotten us, that we
were free to tend our own indwelling light
private & holy
that we would always know each other

by the small fires in our chests

—from *subTerrain*

Hollie Adams

FIVE DAYS A WEEK

the bajillion metal snap-clips in our hair
create a solar flare and our legs
going one
      two three
           one two three
we are fast   how fast?   fast as the dreams
our mothers had on the backs of motorcycles
we are healthy   how healthy?   healthy as a milk
   commercial
starring teens who say no to drugs and yes
to oranges on placemats next to cereal bowls

when our bodies fall out of the sky
no one is alarmed
the middle-aged man with the clicky knee
wants us to fall again
      and again and again and again and again
takes off one giant mitt
to hold in his other giant mitt,
paddles our behinds,   *theatrically*
I am underrotating forever
coming up short   how short?   short as my frou-frou skirt
short as my short program

when the hockey boys get here early
they kill time at Rink B
not looking, we see them through the safety glass
        not looking
the one with the name of a future senator
blond in that evil way
teeth as white   how white?   so white
white as his puka shell necklace
as white as the shutters on a Cape Cod compound
as white as my skates once and
for him I am my electric self
for him my laugh is a clapper-less bell
here is the feeling of being on camera
        and liking it

watch me do my signature move
watch me turn myself into a magic trick
watch me spin so low to the ice   how low?   so low
I could kiss it
so low I could slice off my own nose

afterward we go to Rink A
not looking, they see us through the safety glass
        not looking
shoving each other,   *theatrically*
our moms revving their engines
a convoy of minivans trunks pre-popped
yawning carpeted mouths that ask

aren't you too old for this   how old?   so old
I can do algebra
so young I haven't forgotten it yet

                              —from *Contemporary Verse 2*

Catherine St. Denis

FIVE YEARS AFTER JOE OVERDOSED
ON FENTANYL

In October, I teach the zombie dance
from *Thriller* for PE. (Tweens are fascinated by death
and Michael Jackson, his hilarious pelvis.)
They begin by lying on the varnished floor,
tongues lolling and necks craning, searching out friends
to share mangled pronouncements: *Rlaaaa!*
Urrrrrgh. The beat drops, and then comes the gangly rise

from the grave, all awkward elbows and one-shouldered shrugs.
A synthesized fanfare cues twenty-nine students
to start lurching forward, knees and eyes askew,
the undead in gym shorts and tees, shoelaces bobbing.
They raise clawed hands, and the ones with rhythm
really get it, stomping in circles with leaden calves,
grapevining in lockstep, torsos awry.

And even the kids who mess up look convincing—
a bumbling confusion, the opposition
of bodies controlled by hindbrain viruses,
or adolescence. With all this movement and melody,
with all these pulsing veins of bass, how could they possibly
know how it ends? Sitting on a loveseat

with one arm around your six-year-old,
telling her about Daddy. Wanting
to somehow do it right, as if such news can be
spread gently over a child, like bubbles in the bath.
Should you have turned the television off first?
Never mind. At this point, there will be
few tears. It is not until the cat passes
two years later that the sobs will rise,

fierce and wet. This is how a life ends, spilling
all the way past the rim of time. We were buying
cuffed boots and a Musketeer hat at the thrift shop
as he died. My kid grinned and proclaimed to be using
the "one-tooth maneuver" on her pumpkin that night.
The next morning, Joe's mom slackened
on the sidewalk like a marionette, stringing
her face to the palm of the sky.

He was nowhere. Everywhere. At the winter concert,
our daughter belted "Oh Hannukah," Ethel Merman–style.
Camping, she found a heavy moon snail, held it
rippling in her hands, wondrous, alive. A substitute
teacher insisted she make a Father's Day card.
Our old cat was ailing. The vet prepared the needle
that would uncouple her from her pain. Rising swells
of people uncoupled themselves again and again.

Now in this middle school gym preteens are
mocking death, their tilted grins raised to the ceiling,
their stilted bodies pretending that even after
the gruesome end, there's a hunger that lingers,
a world to upend.

—from *The Malahat Review*

Karen Solie

FLASHLIGHT

In bed near the open window
like someone wandered away from a campfire.

When the eyes adjust
features of the landscape can be discerned

as might the outlines of belief,
no helpful detail within.

When I asked if she'd seen my friend, she said
We don't all know each other in this place

for goodness sake, death is not Saskatchewan.
It's obvious where this is going.

Enough, already, about the soul.
But was it not invented out of the necessity

of a word for the unnecessary
as mathematics needs the null set,

as the flashlight lies beside the bed
though you've lived here long enough

to find your way without it?
There's time enough to tell me that I'm wrong,

she'll do it later.
The prospect that he loved, I see it

and don't see it.
All the things in the night house

as he touches them one by one.
It can be true if you recognize the lie in it, she said.

Far ahead the stubborn soul of my friend
switches off its flashlight,

lays aside its walking stick.
Soon its hands will be free.

It drinks the last of the water
it no longer needs to carry.

—from *The Fiddlehead*

Erin Bedford

FOR MY DAD WHO NEVER READ MY POEMS BUT DIED WITH A WELL-THUMBED COPY OF *WATERSHIP DOWN*

THE JOURNEY

Where are you　　　Far　away
Over　　　the edge of the world.

　　　I will be
　the feathery sky and

the blue and gold of
　spring.
Where are you　　　Far　away

　　　I will be
　the green water and the
　autumn　　　yellow and brown,
the hedge
　　　　Silver

the rain and the berries.

I will be

the deep places

the evening   clouds   red

I am here

O

the heart   the silence

The shining circle

Original text: Silverweed's poem from Richard Adams's Watership Down.

—from *EVENT*

Emily Cann

THE FOX

Pulling the rotted boards up from the deck,
they uncover the carcass of a fox, on its side like a dog
in summer. The opposite of treasure—auburn fur
melting to earth framed by the moss-blackened planks.
They came to do the renovation on the same day
as my procedure. One of them steadied me across
the wound in my deck. The dead fox's empty eye sockets
aimed up my skirt.

In school I held a body
preserved in formaldehyde, veins and arteries stained with dye.
Flesh softer than I expected. Fetal pig skin not at all
the texture of bacon. Tongue lolled out, like he had
died wailing. An artificial stillness
repelling deterioration.

The knife dull and gloved hands awkward,
I pressed the supine limbs open further,
cracking fragile bones and popping joints.
The lights flickered and a boy in the class
snapped my bra strap in the dark.

In a few years I would let him
investigate my ventral side, draw his own
incision down my chest and stomach,

lower—arms out, palms up, as if
awaiting divine repatriation, as if
preparing for him to slip the pins in.
The feeling of skin
carving open. Accommodating indelicacy.
The way I pried the animal apart,
unclasped the body like a purse.

They took the fox away for examination
and replaced the rotten boards with fresh planks
that spring like bungee. The theatre of decay
closed up for the season. The opposite of treasure—
something I never thought of before as empty.

Necropsy is Greek
for sight of death. It is what they will do to the fox to determine
the land I live on is no poison to itself.

Nonviable from the French for *no life*. *Ectopic* Greek
for *out of place*. New boards,
a white searchlight on the deck,
the only evidence of change.

—from *yolk*

Anne Carson

FUNNY YOU SHOULD ASK

How was your trip to New York?
Well,

we stayed at R's. He was away. Asked us to *not* use the sheets—
    quite reasonably,

he has no laundry and who likes coming home to an unclean
bed?

Instructed to bring sheets, we forgot. But try to sleep slightly
above

the sheets, C with his chronic cough, I my insomnia. Wander-
    ing 3 A.M. bedroom

to kitchen I find no teapot, scald myself on the kettle. C still
    coughing, racked,
almost in

tears. Chronic means no one can help. I blunder about, spilling
things

on the floor. Pick up a book I'd thought to read on the plane.
"Hölderlin's

Madness: Chronicle of a Dwelling Life, 1806–1843," by Giorgio Agamben.

It begins with Agamben's exegesis of Hölderlin's critique of Fichte's

understanding of the sentence "I am I." All three have much to say

about this sentence, for "I am I," with its exhilarating syntax and salty

relation of subject to object, does not dispel anyone's tears or blunder,

yet it makes a sort of refuge. Admittedly, I don't quite know who Fichte

is and have to look up *Selbstbewusstsein*, but still, there is a staving

off of terribleness. *To think*. This saving thing. This useless thing. Night

passes, C finally sleeps, Agamben goes on struggling with
   Hölderlin's critique

of Fichte till dawn. My skull sways. "I am I" remains unclarified.

It occurs to me I've spent too much of my life staring at some-
    one else's sentences

in a rebar dawn, measuring my insomnia against their
snap-brim

thoughts. Have I proved a worthy struggler with Agamben's
exegesis

of Hölderlin's critique of Fichte? Not
really.

My mind is
smallish.

Then again, this book of Agamben's was sent me by a former
student,

whose life was changed when he read " . . . in lovely blue . . . "
(Hölderlin,

fragment of a hymn). So (changed) was mine, years ago, I now
    recall. And really,

what more can I ask, whoever I am, of a night on a trip to
New York?

—from *The New Yorker*

Anne Simpson

THE GOLDEN BOAT

—*after Cy Twombly's* Coronation of Sesostris

1

Halfway between where you came from, where
you're headed, in a boat a bed a boat

not meant for this.

A voyage? The question
answered with a circle. Sun, call it,
unseen through the cloud, bits of white velvet.

Is day any different than night?

                  Sleeping: :   :   :   :

those dreams of the burning hut, the cliff
made for falling. What did they give you

for the pain? No glass allowed here,

only plastic. No hangers. Wake
in a hospital, or someone's guest suite, wake

to snow in the elbows of trees, a myth in the early
hours. Ice at the water's edge, one or two
ducks. How easy it is—this pill, that one, the smallest

dawn
dissolving on the tongue.

2

You've slept for years, pills
in the plastic
cup, a boat come from lost, headed
halfway between where you were

and where you are, drifting
into white

velvet, something for the pain, circling, noise
that keeps you up at night,

cells sending
the wrong signals. The red blink,

blink

might be a hidden chariot, a sun,
a cell tower, or crim
son flowerings

of early morning. Red blink. What did they give you
for the pain? Crimson flower

ings of a head

ache. Someone's crying softly, no, whimpering.
Someone's leaving the unit
                                    the door clunks

locks.
Someone's talking outside the locked
door. Red

blink. Some

thing's wrong. The boat's too small,
a tilting cup filled with people.

You wake; you sleep. Another round of pills.

                              —from *The Fiddlehead*

Carolyn Smart

GRIP

After the operation, we slept in separate rooms.
There was a table next to him with medical supplies.
He had a feeding tube that pumped away all night.
I would load the hanging bag with cans of viscous liquid
that would slide into his intestines. In the mornings
I'd flush the tube with water, wash the bags,
sterilize the catheters, do laundry, grind up pills,
think I'm not a fucking nurse but now must act as one.
I felt such relief to tuck him in and shut the light.
I'd go to bed across the hall and read
the only things I could then manage:
Winnie the Pooh, Babar, and a Golden Encyclopedia,
a big green book I loved so much when I was young.
Now I see it filled with colonialism and misogyny.
Once I was small and curious, and the world full of promise.
Nothing that I imagined has come true. Nothing
I could hold onto has stayed. Nothing is the same
including what I find inside these books. Even so
I grip them tightly, as night moves into unimagined day.

—from *Grain*

Y. S. Lee

HE/HIM

   —for J

At seventeen, you almost crashed the Firebird
on a road whose name we've long forgotten.
Flare of yellow in the headlights, then
you stood on the spongy brakes,
wrenched the wheel hard right. We lurched
into stillness, just shy of the ditch

In the minute afterward
engine ticking
cicadas silenced
you asked, *Does life feel real to you now?*
I think I laughed. I definitely thought
No

When you tell me your big news
it's like that moment when the optometrist
flicks one final lever and the soggy letters
suddenly surface, bold and sleek
against a field of light. Oh,
there you are.

                             —from *Grain*

Molly Cross-Blanchard

HERE'S THE THING

Tonight I went to the grocery store for a steak
and on my way dropped the garbage in the garbage
compactor. It was still sunny. I wore shades on my head
and listened to Lizzo while trying to find the bean aisle,
strutted around Buy-Low like the can of cannellinis
were my birthright. Grabbed a cheap red blend
with a twist top, didn't get carded. At home,
with the Burnaby skyline filling all my windows,
I put the popsicles in the freezer, salted the steak
and fed the dog a scoop of kibble. Up to the roof then,
eighteenth-floor metropolitan panorama. There's a garden
and a three-by-five-foot square of my own
possibilities. The carrots had popped up. The marigolds
lost their heads to lucky crows. I borrowed a watering can
from the communal storage box, filled it from a magic spout
in the ground, soaked my seeds. Back downstairs,
steak in the pan with butter and garlic. Chunky yams in the air
fryer. Beyoncé on the Google Home was in the mood
to fuck something up. Tossed arugula with lemon, oil,
parmesan. Watched *White Noise* while I ate,
that new Noah Baumbach, and giggled a lot, said things like
whaaaaaaat and *so cool!* Blood dripped down my chin. The light
left. After, I googled what it all meant—death,
capitalism, Steffie's stuffed bunny—and inevitably
landed on this podcast clip of some porn stars singing

Manuel Ferrara's praises. So right there, on the living room couch
with all those windows open, I watched him tenderly fuck
so many different kinds of women, and I touched myself
and came seven times, and I guess what I've done
tonight is as close to freedom as it gets.
Earlier today a student wrote in an email
you're my favourite prof so maybe that's enough.

—from *Geist*

Molly Peacock

HONEY CRISP

Hello wizenface, hello apple,
understudy in the fridge
since March (it's September).
Hello wrinkly red cheeks,
I'll bet you're almost a year old,
born last autumn,
kept in the fruit storage built
half-underground on the farm,
then, in the snow, sold to me.
Hello my honey crisp (well,
my honey, no longer crisp …),
are you asking why you
haven't been eaten by now?

Because that man hewed to his routines:
an apple for lunch every day,
the same red punctuation.
You were earmarked for the date
he slipped from my arms & we both
slid to the floor, red angel, are you
listening? 911, hospital, hospice,
and ten days later (you were
about six months old then),
he died and was carried
to a cold shelf.

Hello smiley-stem, hello days
moving you from spot to spot.
Hello week where I forgot
and left you at the back and
went about my new life.
Greetings new groceries!
Their jumble causes a re-
arrangement of your bin,
so I have to pick you up
—would you rather
have been eaten and
lived on as energy?
Not yet, not yet, my pomme.
Hello soft wrinkled
face in my palms.

—from *The Walrus*

Pauline Peters

HOUSEBREAKING

And then I want to rise up through the roof
and make my brownskin way
through wood, tile and concrete,
only careful, careful,
like a turtle toothing its way
out of its soft, eggshell home.
I want to rise, rise and stand tall,
head abutting the sun,
arms stretched out to embrace the horizon,
and make my slow bipedal way through the forest,
fingertips stroking the tops of trees,
rain filling the impressions
left by my footsteps,
making new freshwater lakes.
Then I will make my way across the whole of the earth
scooping up borders
and breaking them across my knees.
And when this is done I will rest
in a large body of cool, deep water,
and watch how my knees become
a mountain range covered in trees
and I will lie down in the earth,
and allow the seasons to wash over me
and I will call myself an island,
and I will be welcoming, welcoming.

—from *The Malahat Review*

Elisabeth Blair

A HUNT'S SURVIVING DUCK

is her tufted parallel self

(she grew a garden)

like her
she must start again
in a public pond

(sold ferns at the market)

with nothing but a crust
some stranger tossed

(took money from a hurried man)

who might in other moods
crush her neck
roast her breast

—from *Columba Poetry*

D. A. Lockhart

HUSSAIN RECITES GINSBERG WHILE DRIVING DOWN KEDZIE

Let the sour dampness of this autumn
        night fall into the shell of this rideshare.
        That the dampness of entangled worlds
        collect in unaccelerated air. Open it

with the hesitant chatter of men moving
        between nations, calling clans,
        pathways to names, how one trades
        time for money. In the passing

of storefront signs, traffic between
        neighbourhoods, the seamlessness
        of a city stitched together through
        knowing this to be the static centre.

Hussain is our new millennium surgeon synching
        Ravenswood to Logan Park to Uptown.
        Across from a Vienna Beef dog retaining wall,
        he pauses, glides his sedan to a stop, proclaims

incomparable blind streets of shuddering cloud
        and lightning in the mind leap towards
        poles of Canada & Patterson, illuminating all
        the motionless world of Time between.

The streets before us, his sedan, all beef hotdogs,
        his voice, an intertribal rhapsody drawing
        together where we've been, what we've been
        called, releases them, free, into the city's night air.

—from *EVENT*

Kim June Johnson

I DON'T KNOW WHAT TO DO ABOUT THE WORLD

the robin is pulling a worm   from the ground   & I
have not slept   in this heat   the air   metallic
around me   my eyes blur   on the worm   the bird's
beak   I don't know what to do   about the graves
or the fires   or the children   who are not safe at home
at 3 AM the world is broken   & God   is ludicrous
the earth spins & spins   this morning   the tiny robin
tells me a story   that makes a bit of sense   the dew
that has drawn up food   from the grass   the bird's
well-engineered beak   that knows how   to pull
a worm from the ground   & close by   the river's hush
when the noise   of the neighbour's chain saw   stops
I am not God   I did not make this planet   I just
live here   can it be my job   to love the world
anyway   can I love it   like an old favourite coat
with a torn seam   & missing button?

—from *The New Quarterly*

Amanda Proctor

I FOUND A PLACE WHERE TIME STANDS
STILL

> *In a microscopic description, there can be no sense*
> *in which the past is different from the future.*
>
> —Carlo Rovelli

as a child i roll curlers into grandma's wet hair / pastel and plastic
they resist as i click the pieces together / her hair is so fine i can
see / her scalp it seems translucent like it could tear / when she
is young grandma walks fifty kilometres from mazyr to
potashnya / the smell of gunpowder dust that settles on my
dresser / she walks in the forest off the road away / from the
mines that promise to detonate / dense stars that collapse / she
knows if the soldiers sense something / in the trees they will hear
her movement / as an animal / in her garden the hydrangeas she
plants always bloom blue / spider webs silver between branches
/ proteins glycine or alanine spun / elastic caught in sunlight /
the leaves pull toward the front windows toward the roof / the
spiders will move there even after i've died / as she walks she
does not feel her body sometimes / she thinks of the child she
carries / as she listens to the silence to the fog / to the sound of
rainfall against the leaves / when she reaches her family she
notices / the cuts from the underbrush ribbons / that crisscross
her legs / i put something on the pinewood of her casket / was it
a flower or was it / a fistful of dirt i cannot remember / long
before she is taken her mother bandages / her legs folds a rosary
into her hands / the beads click together between her fingers / at

the border of a black hole time stands still / at the border of a black hole i wrap curlers into grandma's hair / the only way out of the gravitational pull / is to move toward the present / of this moment toward her / soft hair stretched between my fingers

—from *Room*

Domenica Martinello

INFINITY MIRROR

my grandma gongs the gong and is cancer-free
but says she still gets all the perks

a plastic jewel unsews itself from her knock-off
ed hardy cap as the crowd claps and hands her a coffee

someone comes up once a night to wash her back
she throws a bag of cheese curds at the walmart cashier

is honoured in facebook posts
by some of her kids that still speak to her

alive and owning computers
defying all the odds of their childhoods

through the power of pure delusion
she chainsmokes romance novels

I opened one to a random page
found a single grey pubic hair

I was inside her
inside my mom

who was inside with my aunt
who had my cousins inside of her

such is the fuckedupness of biology
all the eggs and follicles

this random magical business
dressed down and destroyed

unsewn from reality
not a gong

or a conjuring
it's a myth in kitsch

no not kitsch
trash

cheap trash
when you're hungry

it's a feast.

—from *Contemporary Verse 2*

Catherine Graham

LAST SHADOW

Flying only happens in dreams.
No one sees the moon-chord

direct the dead through the underground
or bones grip roots.

We lengthen as herons mid-air.
Our past melts yellow for the day's heat cradle.

What holds us back? We count another line
of tin soldiers while buried dolls

do an underground dance.
What once filled sky—never to return—

in a book no reader opens. And yes,
we deleted your voice—regret or let

go—night whistles when the past approaches.
We pollinate sounds through the bee-glade silence

and leave fresh messages to disappear.
Every 'us' must go through it alone. The notion

of guide—futile. We land where we begin—
a hub with no centre to disrobe our last shadow.

—from *Vallum*

Robert Bringhurst

LIFE POEM

—in memoriam Stan Dragland, 1942–2022

Life is language, I wanted to say. Only problem:
it isn't. Not language exactly, not language
as such. Not a particular language either, though
it has a lot to say—in fact, no end of things
to say—and it can listen through the cracks, as every
language needs to do.

Is it something like a language? A metaphor
for language? Or is language a metaphor for it?
Of course, of course. But more like many languages
than one. Like what we call a language
family, which is to say, a swarm—a swarm
in time, in which the living keep on dancing
with the dead because the dead keep flying,
close beside the not-yet-born.

If it were one—the one and only living language—
life wouldn't be alive, or not for long. But swarms
are acrobats in time. They grow, shrink, dodge, feint,
scatter and reform. They have the ears and wings
to do so. Ears enough to constitute a halfway
disembodied mind.

Life heard us coming and will be here watching closely,
hungry, wary, wounded, wordless, like the snakes
of Fukushima and the lynxes of Chernobyl,
when we go—but will not speak of us or curse us
or have any name to give us when we're gone.

Life has been married to language so long that you
might think the two could finish or begin each other's
somersaults and sentences. They don't. It only seems
as if they do. Why? Life is Being discovering
speech. Which is to say Being discovering being.
Is language Being discovering life? It might
be so. Which does not mean that speech
and being are the same.

Language is a sign of life, like swimming, and a form
of life, like eels—but it's not a way of living.
It's also not the life that anything lives—
not even ideas. Your life is not a language,
and your language isn't life. Yet languages
of some kind—nucleic and behavioural,
for instance—are everywhere you listen, look, or rest
your empty hand among the living.

Unspokenness is not life either, but it too
can be a sign of life—just not where there's no hope
of being spoken. Your speechlessness might mean you've dodged
or leapfrogged death, and come, in the desert of words
or the sea of language, to an island
or oasis of not speaking.

The sun's chance in the great celestial darkness
is the snowball's chance in hell. But there it is.
And there, impossibly far off and getting farther,
are the hundred billion galaxies of others,
younger and older, larger and smaller.
Not forever, no, but yes, for the entire
past and future, and for now.

That sun—just one of many, but the only one
there is that is the sun—rains days and nights
on spitted rock and shattered water. Underneath
those fists and hammers, grammars sprout. They crawl
like moss across a lexicon of elements. Not
the celibate elements, no. Not radium,
plutonium, or helium or neon, and not
platinum or gold. The speech palette
and dictionary of life and life-in-waiting
consists of six or ten essential syllables
and twenty-odd occasional inflections.
Some of what-is, that is, is the engine, and some
of what-is is along for the ride.

It's said those elements are lifeless. Yet they speak,
and they are spoken. They have, it's said, a lexicon
and grammar all their own, spun and woven
of electrons, protons, neutrons, which are spun
of something more invisible yet. And is that
everyone's and everything's first language? Every
language's first language? Many languages,
like this one, are intangible. Their phonemes

and their morphemes may be slow—slow as bristlecones, slow
as sequoias—but aren't they still as weightless
as the particles of light?

The sun, in any case, rains down. Atoms bond where they
can bond, and grammars sprout where they can sprout.
Acids, sugars, proteins, fats, and other
phrases, clauses, sentences congeal and then repeat,
repeat. They say what they can say—and sometimes
something more than that. Dancing knee to knee
and toe to toe with others, they carve shapes in space
and time. The shapes are stories. With their borrowed mouths,
the stories drink and feed and lick their wounds and do
their best to reproduce.

And so a language not yet spoken, not yet written,
not yet thought, is caught, or not, between
the carbon and the hydrogen, the phosphorus
and sulfur and the rest of the short list
of what we are and maybe everybody is. And there
it learns, or not, to write, to sing, to talk.

In time, the ones who carry it and feed it start,
or not, to hear what's sung, what's said, to read
what's never more than partly written,
and to talk to what they hear, to say
Yes and, Yes but, and *No,* and more than that.
And more than that.

                    But acrobat
or not, when you have drowned out, hollowed out,

and starved out every language you could find, your own
included, life and death are left with nothing more
to say to you—and no choice but to say it.
Softly at first, in no language at all.
So softly and so plainly and so clearly you
might almost try at first to say it could not,
could not possibly, be you that they are
talking and not talking to.

—from *Brick*

Alison Braid-Fernandez

LIGHT UPON THE BODY

—*after* Luncheon in Room 206 *by Adrienne Dagg*

Next to the mirror in the ferry bathroom was a painting of two girls on a hotel bed. The room was the green I wished I saw on the inside of my eyelids. It was a green that said: *Interior.* How did green—a colour so infrequent to the body, sign of sickness and disease—look so warmly internal? That was the mystery the painting told. Sliced open at the head of the bed was a watermelon baring its softest pink. Looking at it, I was nostalgic for the self before the pain, not this glassy storefront version of me. Over the tinny-sounding speakers came a song that seemed to illuminate the fact that music is noise. What a wonder, I said aloud to the empty stalls, to make noise sound like noise. I wanted to describe the pain I felt in the same illuminating way. The music petered out. Just standing here, I had faced two miracles and remained intact. My body seemed the last mystery to answer. Pain in the body had no image. No outline. My body was in my head. My body was my head. My body was shaking off the rust. My body had grown just a little bit. Had walked through sound and sharp objects. My body was dialogue and forgiveness. My body spelled out desire. Spelled out coincidence. My body was cosmic and grand. My body was my body. My body. My body. I was ice in the tumbler of my body and amber liquid. Held in the bathroom mirror, I chimed and chimed and chimed.

—from *The Adroit Journal*

Evelyn Lau

MINDFUL

—*for Kurt Aydin*

I was coming out of the long darkness
when a streetlight shone on the rain-slick hedge,

and—oh. Green gleam in the corner of my eye,
barbed holly, Chinese jade. Had I held my breath

all winter, blind to beauty? Tonight we contemplate
a dun sesame seed for the count of five—

breath in, out, in. The scarlet stones
that circle your wrist press cool

against the heated thrust of your blood—
a monk's simple beads, when all your life

you've lunged for more, bashing yourself
along the way. Let's say tonight, *this is enough*—

bronze glow in the west, fog slouching south,
bridge visible again. We'll sip priceless tea

from some forgotten village, seek notes
of sticky rice, apple pear, snow leopard—

strain it through our teeth like mud-water.
Pay attention to that first flush of saliva,

the aroma hoarded inside the upturned porcelain lid.
I was drowning in that darkness when all along,

here, this cloud of flowers.

—from *The New Quarterly*

Henry Heavyshield

MY BROTHER, *OM'AHKOKATA* (GOPHER)

My song is the gopher and I am my song.

When I stand on my sentry
stone I see the place
you call home: the yellow fields,
the green hills beyond.

Each day at dusk we play
our underground peoples'
national sport:

The Crossing.

We gather where the grass meets
long-flat-rock. The surface
absorbs the day's heat and in
the waning light warms our paws
and bellies.

Those who aren't playing
come to watch. This is where
we prove ourselves.

The rules are simple:

scurry across long-flat-rock and
hope Bright Eyes doesn't catch you.

During the frozen and slumbering
moons these are the days we
collectively dream about.

Who will prove their bravery?
Whose den will be emptier come fall?

In preparation we feast in the cool
burrows of our clay-bound metropolis.

When runners pass our dens we chirp
them courage songs and wish them
our common blessing: 'may Bright Eyes
leave you spinning but unscathed.'

Spectators carry seeds and flowers.
Gifts for the victorious.
Offerings for the bereaved.

Today I bring my brother his
favourite post-Crossing snack.

Fresh dandelions and a wild rose.

He is the toughest among our clan
and he teases me that only the bravest
ground-swimmers deserve pink flowers.

No one makes me laugh like my
brother. He was born during
a summer of wildfire, when smoke
choked us from the plains and chased
us into the hills.

From the age of a pup he wheezed when
he spoke and wheezed when he laughed.

The night before he had stopped
at my den and asked if I'd join
him during his morning's sentry.

I lied and told him I needed to pick
flowers for that evening's celebrations.
When all I really wanted to do
was return to my dream of roots and
rumours of the ocean below.

Timing. He says the greatest crossers
aren't fast, nor bold, nor nimble,
but they understand timing.

This is his secret. This is his gift.

From the age of pups we learn to speak
the ground's common language.

Anticipation is the rumbling beneath our paws.

My brother waves to us before
dashing to the centre. He stands proud
and he stares Bright Eyes in the face.

She swoops over him and through
the loose grass and dust he remains.

Two more in quick succession.

Whoosh.
Whoosh.

The third staggers him. Dizzy, he
runs away from us and when the fourth
passes over he disappears.

"Brother!" I cry. My clan holds me
back. I swat them with my dandelion and
sprint into the centre of long-flat-rock.

Suddenly there is thunder all around me.
A violent wind. I spin on my back, spared,
breathless.

Standing tall as a sentry I search the gulley.

I call my brother's name.
Louder. Again. Louder.

My clan chirps and whistles but

I cannot hear them. Only the steady
hum. A rumbling through my paws
and my heart is now a one-legged
grasshopper.

"Timing!" someone wheezes from inside
the blowing sage. "Timing!"

I look up. Bright-Eyes barrels
down. I crouch.

Left?

Right?

I sing my clan's name and I run.

—from *The Ex-Puritan*

Rob Winger

NEAR DARK PARK

> *So / much of America belongs to the trees.*
> —Ada Limón

I was steering the rental car through hillside Larkspur side streets, and it was raining again, so your job was to point out wonders: the shining flood streaming over tidy pavement, a wartime postage-stamp lot filled with manicured bamboo and lemon trees, this shaded plastic playground, complete with free public washrooms built in handsome cabins, all of it set in the dark hold of a second-growth redwood grove lined with curving bike lanes and well-trained Labradors.

One avenue later, we found it, framed in a raised, custom-made bed that was maybe six feet square but angled into a cutwater diamond, set right inside the left lane: a fifty-foot tree, saved. It might have been an oak or an acacia or some other California local. Or it might have been, like us, a legal alien. We didn't take pictures. Our phones were in our pockets.

In the dark, the lip of its bed was smooth concrete, the same stuff poured to mark a roadside limit, and we beheld, breathless, the way its resting place was let to live there inside the middle of things, as though it had that right, as though it still belonged. Someone had planned and fought for this, we said, had convinced transportation committees or battled civic bylaws. Someone had won.

We seemed to hover there. We clapped our hands and went teary eyed, thinking there might be hope after all, despite our silver strip mines. We wanted this tree to feel us feeling this, were hoping it was happy to be there in light traffic, glad to greet each resident who might pat its gnarled bark en route to downtown street lights, to rest, an easy introvert sticking to the safe corners of all our daily dusk parties.

But what does it mean to save a single cathedral from a whole city of cathedrals? To carry to the clean air just one of the kids stuck in a burning schoolhouse?

Stubborn, sure-footed, stained-glass green, we said to the tree, *please tell us all of it's true*: that each rocket's shimmering velocity depends on fuming contrails, that the aluminum-foil litter shining in the river looks angelic to every spawning salmon, that the dirty cobalt that makes possible Siri's gleaming touch screen was carried here through gorgeous tides and sunsets to be installed on purpose in our dry suburban cabin, thousands of clever engine parts working in communion underneath our hood to set aflame the ancient fluids we've lifted through caprock to pull us here to this exact address.

Outside, our wipers calmly obliterate each raindrop blessing the sloped windshield. You reach past the gearshift to cup your palm across my forearm. We're both alive, you say, or maybe don't. Inside, I turn the dry wheel into breeze and fog and scented blooms, every steadfast steering column, only clumsy luck.

—from *Brick*

Evelyna Ekoko-Kay

ON MY SHOULDERS

my autism is a disruption
to the ordinary body-

mind relationship. I know
what I should do I know how I should

sound I know the ways you want
my legs to bend, my gaze to pierce,

my cadence to unravel.
I know I am annoying you.

I know there is a circle
made of people talking softly

looking at each other.
I am trying to be a person

in the circle, just another
talking body, meeting eyes

and saying "fine, and you?"
I stand in the circumference

and the circle tightens,
leaving me behind.

I try to get a shoulder in.
everyone else manages

to slot in like a flock of geese
returning in formation

from the south. they are not touching.
there should be a space for me

but I can't get a shoulder in.
am standing just behind

their backs blocked out like actors
in a dress rehearsal

performing their lines perfectly.
when I did theatre

I could never find the light.
the crew would get frustrated.

"just walk forward 'til you feel it"
they would tell me.

"you should feel it."
I'm told the light is hot.
I performed my scenes in partial
darkness, never knowing

if I could be seen. I don't know
why. it was just a spotlight.

just a glowing circle on the floor.
I can't feel the light.

I can always feel the light.
I know how light should feel.

—from *The Ex-Puritan*

Jaeyun Yoo

ORCHIDS

Once, there was a woman
who escaped a serial killer
by admiring his magenta orchids.
How do you keep them in bloom?
        Two ice cubes in the pots per week,
        west-facing windows, perlite soil.
How does somebody like you
end up kidnapping a woman?
She brewed him a cup of chamomile tea
while he blubbered sob stories about his mother.
She patted his back, a princess kissing
a bulbous toad to lift an ancient curse. He let her go.
She bolted barefoot to the nearest store,
a barber shop with chipped checkerboard tiles
and hair piled like mildew. She called 911.
I hate these kinds of urban myths—
should a woman's survival
rely on luck, sainthood sympathy,
outwitting a soft fool, or else, blood?
I want to hear about how nothing happens
when walking alone, earbuds playing ABBA,
through a park dim as a beer bottle.
She returns home to her houseplants
sprays them three times for a good night.

—from *Contemporary Verse 2*

Alexander Hollenberg

ORIGIN STORY, WITH CROW

—on the occasion of Earth Day 2023

The crow's wing is a blade
slicing the ocean open:

inside, the usual offal—birds' nests
of old transatlantic cable, fists of seagrass

that clasp and conceal the bleached bones
of tankers and trawl nets, dusky shards of fallen stars

set down on the seabed in a sunken syzygy
of celestial trash—a drowned, stationary orbit.

Even deeper in abyssalpelagic space, a forest
of grey spruce slow-dances

in the dark undercurrent, like phosphenes
forged by the pressure of water and salt.

The crow plucks one, squirrels it in her plumage
and soars—for a moment spruce and crow and sea and sky

concatenate, which is to say create,
a new cosmos in the ink of her wing,

connecting the drowned
to what cannot be drowned.

She returns the spruce to drier ground, from its boughs
watches fishermen gadding about the bright, boatless harbour,

gathering bait and gossip, mending generations
of decay in their nets,

listens to them quiz one another about traps and tides,
the topography of a good trawl line, the boundaries

of inherited territories and the brisk profits
to which they'll one day return—

as if returning
is something that will always happen,

as if there were a net wide enough
to reel back in the world.

—from *Contemporary Verse 2*

Bertrand Bickersteth

A POEM ABOUT BLACKBOY'S HORSE

Boy's horse stepped in a badger's hole, lost her footing
and fell. Boy was flipped

in the air. His foot caught in the stirrup. He felt a pain
shoot through his ankle,

felt the inertia of his flight take over the topography, twist
westerly, still tilting to the east.

His body was a loose spigot pivoting around the fulcrum
of a meaningless ankle.

He felt his fingers slipping through her withers, felt the fear
of the horse rushing to the ground

above him. He couldn't stop any of it. Couldn't stop himself
from imagining the unknowable

impact or the whistle of weight to follow. He knew what was
coming. He knew the soil

he was headed for. Knew its knowledge. The chemistry of
its creativity: mildly gleysolic

chernozem, churning life and his livelihood as he knew it.
Knew it, too, as foreign, as far

from familiar as he was from family. He tried to imagine a family
but their image burst into the falling

air before him, before fading, as always, into the darkness
of dirt. Then came the weight

of sadness and the piercing pain of the forgone, unmentioned,
unmurmured, like that flash of green,

that patch of wild timothy whose individual blades know nothing
of their shared past,

know nothing of their sibling entanglement, nothing at all
of their intertwined roots

whose domain is the catacombs beneath the crust, whose action
is downward groping, like fingers of ancestry,

a blind quest in the sorrow of soil, forever fumbling, forever
    finicking
for the unknowable mother of darkness.

—from *The Fiddlehead*

Fareh Malik

PRAISE US, FOR WE ARE DEAD

An imam shouts over   bullhorn feedback,   and broadcasts
that   we need to welcome and provide for   a new Pakistani
family in the area.   When it's Jummah in the summer heat
lamp suns strike the back   of prostrated necks—   sweat
communes   and   rolls off skin   smoother than slurs off
lips   as you   leave the Islamic centre parking lot.   A holy
perspiration   crashes   in   the   middle of   janamaz
fibres   flooding a crater   cast by your forehead.
Sit   up,   set   your   gaze   down, tell me;   wasn't
every ocean first just   an earthly wound,   we   bandaged
with moisture? An incision we have   cried above   until   we
could   swim it   end-to-end?   Aren't we all just   trying
to make torn flesh   whole again? The carpet in the prayer rug,
now   saturated—   wet   and   salty   as the
Clifton shore.   This is a   small act of your body   trying
to   give someone   a home   that they no longer
have.   The next week, uncle   breaks shoulder-to-shoulder
silence with his cracking joints;   strained knees   listen
to a khutba   about partitions. A   sermon   honouring the
dead   halfway around the world—   the ground splits   open
and   tombstones erect in the middle of the masjid,   but my
family still can't   find   our ancestors'   graves
in Pakistan.   Sometimes ghosts are   the   realest piece of
something   we have left.   This poem   is about losing

97

a home,   and trying to find it,   and failing,   and surviving,
and building,   and having to   house its haunting.

—from *The Ex-Puritan*

Armand Garnet Ruffo

RESTING II

See the hidden graves
between the trees,
    the unmarked ones,
    the ones that will be forever nameless,
the children are resting.
Resting? As if each child
were tucked in
with a lullaby, a teddy bear,
a goodnight kiss.

It isn't true. Where do the lies
come from? They are not resting.
Though we do what we can for them,
pray, sing, put down tobacco,
burn sweetgrass and sage,
watch little hearts of smoke
curling up towards the sky.

Listen, they are below our feet.
Can you hear them?
Their tiny bones
are turning as we speak,
turning to dust
turning to soil
turning to plants and animals,

in turn turning.
Look there, carefully,
over by that mound
barely noticeable under the damp leaves.
You can see their thin arms
tendrils of green
reaching
twisting
pushing
up through the earth.

—from *Arc Poetry Magazine*

Kayla Czaga

SAFE DESPAIR

Because she could not stop for Death,
Death drove alongside, shouting—
Emily, get in the car.

Death said Emily seemed older, closer to his age.

When Death slid into Emily's DMs, did he send:
a) threats
b) eggplant emojis
c) obscure Slovenian poetry
d) links to news articles
   in which he featured prominently
e) grim reaper tattoos with
   How about my face on your bicep, baby?
   Just you, me, and Immortality.

Death said Emily was different.
Emily said that was *so Death.*
Their conversations went: *Death,*
Death, Death, Death, Emily, Death.

For their one-month anniversary
Death bought Emily a birch-white box,
five and a half feet long with pewter knobs.

Emily's journal entries went: Death—
Death—Death—Death—Homework—Death.

Death tutored Emily in physics. For instance,
if Death dropped Emily off the steeple,
he knew the impact would snap her neck.

Death knew all about things like physics,
obscure knots, nu metal, and what living
girls were like, what they liked.

Death said dead girls didn't understand him.
Only Emily could understand him.

Only Emily and her meters of lace,
museum of ceramic feelings, her breath
flogging the pane and long trembling
fingers could understand him.

Late at night, Death read a poem to Emily
over the phone that made her bones glow.

On weekends she visited the hospital cafeteria
where he spooned corn and wore a hairnet.
She ate Jell-O and acted incurably.

Death said there were opportunities
for him in the city. Did Emily think
his denim professional?

Emily stared out into the peppy blue Amherst light,
which only understood different forks
and how to hold them. It made her tired.
In her notebook, she wrote, D+E 4eva
&eva—and meant it.

Death got hired doing security at a bank,
buzzed his head, bought a tie and looked alive.

He said, *I am lifting weights now.*
I am feeling so powerful.

He said, *Our connection*
is too special for monogamy.

Emily's journal entries went: Death—Death—
Death—Emily—see I am doing better—
Death—soon I will be ok—Death—
Death + Emily—Death − Emily =
I will never understand physics so long
as I live—Death. Amherst blows.

Death said, *I'll visit next weekend,* as weekends
piled up in pages on Emily's desk,
and she circled *all of the above* on every test.

Emily believed her breathing would take
forever to get normal. She made horizontal
marks in the margins of her arms.

She folded her notebook pages into coffins
and cranes until she felt a formal
purple purging in her veins.

—from *The Malahat Review*

Cassidy McFadzean

STORM KING

The citizens of this land build massive sculptures
to honour the king   And when he is pleased he shows mercy
And if he is displeased he rouses a hurricane
At very end of our trip it was supposed to rain but didn't
We approached *Wavefield* but didn't walk on the wave
We lay by a wall of stone where I read to you "Mending Wall"
And after weeks of discomfort, finally cracked my back
At home I bathed in the green copper water
I asked what you were building and you said *context*
We should think of each day as having twelve rounds
I'm tired of feeling things in my body   Like ions
All the apartment's doorknobs have been removed
The last tenant afraid of being locked inside
In a house with no exits   It's details that frustrate:
That my mother described her symptoms to a pharmacist
concerned they were a side effect of medication
(she was having the heart attack that killed her)
I stare into middle distance as defence mechanism
(so I don't get attacked on the subway again)
Fear manifests as compulsion   Where is the feeling
I used to have (that life was taking place)

—from *long con magazine*

Erín Moure

THE STRAYING OF ALL TRANSLATION:
A PHRASE ARCHIVE

The Straying of All Translation / O que non quere cesar de mover

From: x~~█████~~@gmail.com
Subject:
Date: April 24, 2022 at 1:06 PM
To: Erín Moure

Its from downfall that we arise.

It is downfall that founds us.

It is from downfall that we rise up

It is in foundering that we are founded

It is in collapse that we are founded

Whoosh from my iPhone

Ultimately, it is collapse that gives us our foundation

It is, in short, the foundering that founds us.

It is in the very foundering that we find new foundation.

Our foundation is this very foundering.

"Ultimately, in foundering we found ourselves anew"
"It is in foundering that we find foundation"
"The foundering is that which founds us."
"It is the foundering that founds us."

"En definitiva é o abatemento o que nos funda"

« Or c'est en définitive l'effondrement qui nous fonde. »
(corrected from p. 101 of the all too human virus) ^{Jean-Luc Nancy}

—from *Polyglot*

Eve Joseph

SUPERPOWERS

When I wasn't looking the broken bowl repaired itself. The genie
let himself out of the bottle. The tide retreated so far back I could
see yesterday. In the interval when I looked away the dog with
three legs grew a fourth and did backflips on the trampoline. I
tested my new powers by blindfolding myself. Sure enough,
overnight Ponge, Follain, and Jacob showed up like elves in the
shoemaker's shop and in the morning the table was piled high
with poems written on blue sheets of paper. Wow! I wondered
how far I could take this. What would happen if I looked? This
is the point where it can all go wrong. Where the gift of the poem
gets weighted down by craft. Take away the wind and the clouds
will have to row themselves across the sky.

—from *Arc Poetry Magazine*

Sue Goyette

SURPRISE: AN ARMOIRE (IN A SUNNY SPOT, I'M HOPING)

Mother of pearl glare. Tongue spiced by glove pulled off by
   teeth. Birthing.

She was the first elevator I got into. Sonically unnerving, my
   mother's nervous system

was a hospital corridor. We must've frolicked before I was born

in the old-fashioned way—all ice cubes and decor. This is when
   I truly knew her.

I'd follow her into the cloakroom to ask: *but are you sure?*

The most unexpected thing about grief is how she turned up as
   an armoire

delivered to a neighbour's house wrapped up in a thick blanket
   and carried

actively, as in *being cared for.* Glass got broken in her previous
   life.

Before she died voluptuously. Taking in the weather like a
   respirator.

I can only imagine how heavy a trail that thunder made the
   night she died

and how she'd have to heft it like a wet boa over her shoulder as
   she left.

I spice her with way more attitude than she ever had. Except in
   the last two of weeks

of her life. Then she was as brash as a ship leaving port. For
   god's sake, she said

in a dream, am I too over the top, wanting a *partay* with fancy
   sandwiches?

I didn't expect the breach and rip, the inverse of birthing. How
   my body feels

ravaged by her passing through me and I didn't expect the
   comfort I sometimes feel

when a molecule of her good self melts on me like a snowflake.

This is an alert thirst. And the last brave stand of being a
   daughter. Who knows what

chicanery she can get up to now that her energy is all disassem-
   bled and free.

O little tumbleweed. O little ash. These deep breaths in are my
   paltry attempts

to keep the new versions of you close. And this getting on my
   knees may look like drama

but the feeling is the realest I've been.

—from Arc Poetry Magazine

David Martin

TINNITUS

My ear is humming a song that lasts all night
and day. The song has one note, and it never
varies in rhythm or tempo: fermata forever
waiting for its conductor to end the plight.
You might be thinking this pitch is like a bite,
and that I spend my hours wishing to sever
the roar, or trick it with something very clever
to shut it up and stop the dissonant fight.
But I don't mind this vexing cry of wind
(much) anymore that's caught inside my head,
a reminder that my every thought is sonic.
The words I speak are pedal-pointed, pinned
to this song that will be with me till I'm dead,
a single tone that's stretched for me, my tonic.

—from *Poetry Pause*

Gerald Hill

TO CELEBRATE WAVES RIGHT TO LEFT IN A SHIRT-RIPPLING WIND, TAVIRA, PORTUGAL

Lying on the sand you'd burn eventually, get thirsty.
You'd peel and eat your apple. You'd try
for a moment to name what the waves think
they're doing, you'd ask the same of yourself,
why not. You'd flex your body on a bed of fine sand.
You'd find so many shells your hands
tingle when you walk. You wouldn't dig far for dampness.

So the world begins and ends in *sky, sea, sand*
not forgetting sun breathing fragments of cloud
or yourself giving birth to this.

—from *Grain*

Tolu Oloruntoba

"UNDERSTAND ME, LOVE ME, ANSWER ME": 77 QUESTIONS FROM ANNE SZUMIGALSKI

who are we?[1]
who am i?[2]
who was i?[3]
i am?[4]

self, self, what self is that?[5]
what good is that to me? [6]
who is the enemy? [7]
and who will listen? [8]
when you knock will anyone open the door?[9]
and if they do listen, who will believe you? and... [10]
... if they believe you, who will care? [11]

who who who?[12]
do you imagine you're making a new claim
        to earth's old journey? [13]
who will knit up these strands of thought and power
        into a web of memory? [14]
what have we left to us   at our age?[15]
what was it that we suffered   that we shared?[16]
can you survive all this?   can i? [17]

well my dear are you wondering
why i tell these bizarre stories?[18]
remember the plague-cart trundling in the street? [19]
can we remember the future?[20]
how we dashed in with cloths over our faces?[21]
we didn't ask why this one was wet at the crotch,

      why that one lay clutching a bundle of herbs.[22]
is this memory? is this invention?[23]
what was it? ...   where was it?[24]
... can there be two sides to a question you are arguing

       with yourself?[25]
how many steps to the reinvention of memory?[26]
is distance itself the sound of the word—distance, distance?[27]
is this the hurricane of the mind which breaks light

      from light from light

      and becomes darkness?[28]
do we invent the memories of our foremothers?[29]

---

those in power have always played fast and loose with the rest
   of us,

      haven't they?[30]
does nothing ever really change for any of god's creatures?[31]
we are born into a dancing biosphere.

      Shall we stand still then and deny it?[32]

our first gods were fishes, for how could we not worship

      the elegance of their ribs

      the economy of their entrails?[33]

tell me what you imagine encloses the ecosphere,
      indeed the universe?
      daughter, there is a nightgown for everything. [34]
it's true, isn't it, that to return to god is to come back to oneself? [35]
it's true, isn't it, that before something has become a whole
      we may not refer to it as divided? [36]
what colour then is the inner being of a shining angel? [37]
have you noticed how they roost in trees? [38]
how do i explain my love for this small but uppity thing? [39]
my darling seedling will you flourish? [40]

what is a man to do when the tree he loves is rotting at its centre?
      what is a woman to do when the man she loves is pale
      as a sickly tree? [41]
After all why should we debase ourselves simply to please a
    power-hungry old man? [42]
be ashamed, o god, be ashamed of your dryness, your lack of
    words.
      how is it that the very wind speaks,
      but you do not answer us? [43]
(what else is there to say?) [44]

---

what are words, what are words after all?
      can words free us? can words kill our enemies?
      can a word become a knife to stab the oppressor? [45]
the interior sounds the body makes—how do they escape
      to the outside air, to ears other than our own,
      though we try to close every orifice? [46]

who is to blame for my lip's blisters?[47]
and what has this to do with poetry being a virus?[48]
what's this curling murderously around my neck?[49]
the fear of death that will not let you rest,
        the even greater fear of immortality?[50]
are we most ourselves or the second skins we slough off
        as poems?[51]
will there ever be a day when we understand
        numbers, where they start
        and how they flourish and fade?[52]
the question is which
        of these days was first
        which will be the last?[53]
what difference will it make?[54]
and the altered mind of the artist, the poet, is this caused by
        a chemical imbalance?[55]
how in fact, did we come to write anything…?[56]
wasn't there a rumour just lately though that a virus,
        this very virus of poetry, perhaps,
        was about to destroy the world and inherit the earth?[57]
shall we burn our mushroom to a cloud of smoke?[58]
will that do?[59]

---

i have so much to tell you   will you or won't you hear   my
    confession?[60]
how to begin a story at the end, when the battle is fought and lost,
        and crows are picking the bones of all flesh?[61]
i'm not even sure that i want to survive, to go on, to what?[62]

there was no road and no direction.

  would there ever be again?[63]

how many hours, how many days of this?[64]

what's a life without purpose?[65]

is this the invention of memory—the reinvention?[66]

but is this all? of course not.[67]

are you then everything there is?[68]

why won't somebody understand me?

  am i speaking in an unknown tongue?

  understand me, love me, answer me.[69]

       —from *Prairie Fire*

Carmelita McGrath

VISIT, JULY 25, 2020

The boy arrives at 2:25 am;
like most things here the visit is random.
Let's call him G., I have no right to his whole name
and as I write, wonder if I should tell more
than that he's looking for a light. Which I give him.
But there is more because he wants more, needs more.
Can he sit and smoke his cigarette? For sure.
He sits and I see his eyes sidle toward my glass of wine.
Does he want some? His gratitude far exceeds
both intent and offer, the wine, the water.
G. says he's waiting until the worst of the night
settles itself into pre-dawn quiet before finding
the most promising of unpromising spaces to lay
his pack down, his head, the little flesh that shields his bones.
Leukemia, he says, since he was twelve, in remission
when his parents decided they didn't want him
under their roof after his first breaking free.
But now. Well, that explains his preternatural thinness,
his pallor cut by angles of shadows
so much so that when he appeared I imagined
one turned by a vampire in pre-adolescence.
But no. He's twenty-eight, homeless these ten years.
I see him, before he leaves, glance through the patio doors
to the candlelit kitchen, maybe thinking I'm lucky.
Let him think so. Let me imagine so, if only

for a little while tonight, that I have found my space, my peace.
Let me forget on the slightest of evidence that this place,
a decommissioned backpacker's Airbnb,
was all I could find when Covid hit, all I could afford,
all I could muster after the hopeless search for work,
after the eviction, a few treasures stored, the rest on the street.
Let me forget how I saw my life bagged in black plastic
looking through the window when I went to collect mail.
The plants dying. No access, a brutally cold night.
January. And now exactly six months later. Imagine
that this garden I planted on a concrete slab,
the nasturtiums golden, the waving cosmos,
the squeeze of freshly watered rosemary and lemon thyme,
pressed to my face. Imagine this small comfort
between the new moon and first quarter as larger, the way
the moon waxes. Imagine that I don't now share this space
with the drug dealer in the front room, the deaf DJ king
of Montreal deafening the neighbours in reciprocity. Imagine I
    don't hear
him yelling orders to his minions who haul gear for him, who
    dress like him,
as they trundle huge speakers down the hall. Par-ty! Par-ty!
How are you here, one of the lost boys asked, newly arrived
    from France
thinking he'd found rastas, ending up among the skinheads.
Well, I could say, if my French were better, you are not where you
travelled to either. Failure to be clear is more than a language
    barrier.
Imagine that later, earlier, when the sky begins to bloom, coral,

there won't be rats in the kitchen, one scrabbling with its sharp
    claws
in the wall of the bedroom, chewing on the plaster,
drawn from the alley where the garbage piles up.
My *ruelle verte* one side of the concrete slab. Imagine that the DJ's
new girlfriend, lover of cocaine, budgetarily downsized to crack,
won't fall to pieces, a broken doll on the bathroom floor, putting
her legs back on in slow motion. Imagine that, this day last week,
I didn't have my sixtieth birthday here. Another week, I'll mark
it again, somewhere else, temporary for sure, but better.
Go ahead now, say what you're thinking: that woman is crazy
or resilient. And let me tell you, they're the same thing.
Resilience has its limits; I hope you never find them.

—from *Riddle Fence*

Kate Genevieve

WHEELS ON THE BUS GO

Remember when we pulled their bodies from
under piles of skin and cotton, the way their

wrists left the sockets on the final tug, but we
popped 'em back in, folded their arms through

cartoon backpack straps and brought them
home midday to wash their faces clean, rusty

blood circling around and around—or is it again
and again—down the drain. Remember how,

after supper, we tucked them into floral pyjamas
and flannel bedspreads, turned on little lights so

they wouldn't lie in the dark. Remember how, in
the morning, we propped them up at tables and fed

scrambled eggs to slackened lips, slid the spoon along
cheeks instead, eggs tumbling onto kitchen tiles.

Remember how it was too late, but we slipped those
little feet into light-up Skechers, filled yellow busses

with bodies, and kept sending them back again and again.

—from *The Malahat Review*

Ronna Bloom

WHERE I'VE BEEN

I've been to where the sky picked me up like Dorothy
and took me to a diner. It was kinder than a hurricane
but blew black. I've been to panic and back
several times a day on the no-go bus. I've been freaked.
I've been to the doctor, the doctor, to medical imaging twice.
I've been to the phone when it rings and when it sits there.

I've been to bed. I've bitten fear into hunger and sadness.
I've been too crazy for words. I've been without them. And with.
And missing. I've been waking up and waking up
scared. I've been reactive and grounded. Sober
and sober and drunk. Wandering.

This morning early, as the feelings started pouring in
while the awareness was still bright, I saw
how ordinary it is/I am to have all these feelings. However
    dramatic.
They cruise across like a kite surfer while I watch from the shore.
No. I am flying, and surfing, and crossing. How it just
goes and goes. When the kite surfer fell, I fell
I was what was left: the wake, the waking, the water.

—from *Canthius*

Sara Truuvert

YOU GREW AN ORANGE

Taking God at his word is a choice,
you taught your Sunday school students
& it kicked you out of church. While everyone
laughed at some blind men groping at an elephant,
you approached each one to listen to him sing of a rope,
a tree, a wall so huge it made him weep. Losing a mother,
a father, a sister, brother, wife, son & still you keep your heart awake
to drive me to the zoo.
Last year, another gentle rebellion—you grew an orange
in your apartment, in frozen Toronto. Surprised,
it softened & thrived bold enough to eat
on your astounded table.

—from *The Fiddlehead*

NOTES

"UNDERSTAND ME, LOVE ME, ANSWER ME":
77 QUESTIONS FROM ANNE SZUMIGALSKI

1   Szumigalski, A. (1997). Victim. In *On glassy wings* (p. 94). Coteau Books.

2   Szumigalski, A. (1997). Victim. In *On glassy wings* (p. 94). Coteau Books.

3   Szumigalski, A. (1997). Victim. In *On glassy wings* (p. 94). Coteau Books

4   Szumigalski, A., & Abley, M. (2006). A Conversation. In *When Earth leaps up* (p. 73). Brick Books

5   Szumigalski, A., & Abley, M. (2006). A Catechism (or Conversation). In *When Earth leaps up* (p. 60). Brick Books.

6   Szumigalski, A. (1997). Long Distance. In *On glassy wings* (p. 85). Coteau Books.

7   Szumigalski, A. (1997). The Name of our City. In *On glassy wings* (p. 114). Coteau Books.

8   Szumigalski, A. (1995). In *Z: A meditation on oppression, desire and freedom* (p. 31). Coteau Books.

9   Szumigalski, A. (1997). Paradijslaan. In *On glassy wings* (p. 159). Coteau Books.

10 Szumigalski, A. (1995). In *Z: A meditation on oppression, desire and freedom* (p. 31). Coteau Books.

11 Szumigalski, A. (1995). In *Z: A meditation on oppression, desire and freedom* (p. 31). Coteau Books.

12   Szumigalski, A. (1995). In *Z: A meditation on oppression, desire and freedom* (p. 23). Coteau Books.

13   Szumigalski, A. (1997). On The Sun. In *On glassy wings* (p. 173). Coteau Books.

14   Szumigalski, A., & Abley, M. (2006). Statement: Reinventing Memory. In *When Earth leaps up* (p. 41). Brick Books.

15   Szumigalski, A. (1986). Want Of [b] Want Of [D]. In *Dogstones: Selected and new poems* (p. 74). Fifth House.

16   Szumigalski, A. (1986). Want Of [b] Want Of [D]. In *Dogstones: Selected and new poems* (p. 74). Fifth House.

17   Szumigalski, A. (1997). The Arrangement. In *On glassy wings* (p. 122). Coteau Books.

18   Szumigalski, A. (1986). A Midwife's Story Three. In *Dogstones: Selected and new poems*. Fifth House.

19   Szumigalski, A., & Abley, M. (2010). On Wildfire. In *A peeled wand: Selected poems* (p. 57). essay, Signature Editions.

20   Szumigalski, A., & Abley, M. (2006). Statement: Reinventing Memory. In *When Earth leaps up* (p. 41). Brick Books.

21   Szumigalski, A., & Abley, M. (2010). On Wildfire. In *A peeled wand: Selected poems* (p. 57). Signature Editions.

22   Szumigalski, A., & Abley, M. (2010). On Wildfire. In *A peeled wand: Selected poems* (p. 57). Signature Editions.

23   Szumigalski, A., & Abley, M. (2006). Statement: Reinventing Memory. In *When Earth leaps up* (p. 40). Brick Books.

24   Szumigalski, A. (1990). Night Terrors, Night Solaces. In *The word, the voice, the text: The life of a writer* (p. 95). Fifth House.

25   Szumigalski, A. (1990). The Joy of Contention. In *The word, the voice, the text: The life of a writer* (p. 32). Fifth House.

26   Szumigalski, A., & Abley, M. (2006). Statement: Reinventing Memory. In *When Earth leaps up* (p. 40). Brick Books.

27 Szumigalski, A. (1997). On Loneliness. In *On glassy wings* (p. 81). Coteau Books.

28 Szumigalski, A., & Abley, M. (2006). You and I at the Rapids. In *When Earth leaps up* (p. 30). Brick Books.

29 Szumigalski, A., & Abley, M. (2006). Statement: Reinventing Memory. In *When Earth leaps up* (p. 41). Brick Books.

30 Szumigalski, A. (1990). The Poetry Game. In *The word, the voice, the text: The life of a writer* (p. 49). Fifth House.

31 Szumigalski, A., & Abley, M. (2006). A Herring Lives in the Sea. In *When Earth leaps up* (p. 64). Brick Books.

32 Szumigalski, A. (1990). On Gesture. In *The word, the voice, the text: The life of a writer* (p. 73). Fifth House.

33 Szumigalski, A., & Abley, M. (2010). Our First Gods Were Fishes. In *A peeled wand: Selected poems* (p. 77). Signature Editions.

34 Szumigalski, A., & Abley, M. (2006). A Conversation). In *When Earth leaps up* (p. 73). Brick Books.

35 Szumigalski, A., & Abley, M. (2006). A Catechism (or Conversation). In *When Earth leaps up* (p. 60). Brick Books.

36 Szumigalski, A., & Abley, M. (2010). i2 = -1. In *A peeled wand: Selected poems* (p. 84). Signature Editions.

37 Szumigalski, A. (1997). On The Nature & History of Angels. In *On glassy wings* (p. 204). Coteau Books.

38 Szumigalski, A., & Abley, M. (2010). Angels. In *A peeled wand: Selected poems* (p. 74). Signature Editions.

39 Szumigalski, A. (1997). Malus. In *On glassy wings* (p. 196). Coteau Books.

40 Szumigalski, A. (1997). Malus. In *On glassy wings* (p. 196). Coteau Books.

41 Szumigalski, A. (1997). What Is a Man to Do. In *On glassy wings* (p. 193). Coteau Books.

42 Szumigalski, A. (1997). Gerald. In *On glassy wings* (p. 135). Coteau Books.

43 Szumigalski, A. (1997). Purple. In *On glassy wings* (p. 175). Coteau Books.

44 Szumigalski, A. (1986). The Portrait of E. In *Dogstones: Selected and new poems* (p. 46). Fifth House.

45 Szumigalski, A. (1995). In *Z: A meditation on oppression, desire and freedom* (p. 4). Coteau Books.

46 Szumigalski, A. (1997). The Cranes. In *On glassy wings* (p. 43). Coteau Books.

47 Szumigalski, A. (1997). Childermas Three. In *On glassy wings* (p. 69). Coteau Books.

48 Szumigalski, A. (1990). Is Poetry a Virus? In *The word, the voice, the text: The life of a writer* (p. 42). Fifth House.

49 Szumigalski, A. (1997). Woman Reading in Bath. In *On glassy wings* (p. 129). Coteau Books.

50 Szumigalski, A. (1990). Night Terrors, Night Solaces. In *The word, the voice, the text: The life of a writer* (p. 97). Fifth House.

51 Szumigalski, A. (1997). Don Kerr's Foreword. In *On glassy wings* (p. iii). Coteau Books.

52 Szumigalski, A. (1997). Theirs is The Song. In *On glassy wings* (p. 2). Coteau Books.

53 Szumigalski, A., & Abley, M. (2010). Old Woman in Winter. In *A peeled wand: Selected poems* (p. 55). Signature Editions.

54 Szumigalski, A., & Abley, M. (2006). A Conversation). In *When Earth leaps up* (p. 72). Brick Books.

55 Szumigalski, A. (1990). Night Terrors, Night Solaces. In *The word, the voice, the text: The life of a writer* (p. 96). Fifth House.

56 Szumigalski, A. (1990). Introduction. In *The word, the voice, the text: The life of a writer* (p. 12). Fifth House.

57 Szumigalski, A. (1990). Is Poetry a Virus? In *The word, the voice, the text: The life of a writer* (p. 44). Fifth House.

58 Szumigalski, A. (1997). Ergot and After. In *On glassy wings* (p. 79). Coteau Books.

59 Szumigalski, A. (1990). Blake's White. In *The word, the voice, the text: The life of a writer* (p. 100). Fifth House.

60 Szumigalski, A. (1997). Sitting Under Death's Rich Shade. In *On glassy wings* (p. 117). Coteau Books.

61 Szumigalski, A., & Abley, M. (2010). Voice. In *A peeled wand: Selected poems* (p. 41). Signature Editions.

62 Szumigalski, A. (1995). In *Z: A meditation on oppression, desire and freedom* (p. 51). Coteau Books.

63 Szumigalski, A., & Abley, M. (2010). Viaticum—The Text. In *A peeled wand: Selected poems* (p. 71). Signature Editions.

64 Szumigalski, A. (1997). Making Up a Four. In *On glassy wings* (p. 108). Coteau Books.

65 Szumigalski, A. (1997). Videotape. In *On glassy wings* (p. 15). Coteau Books.

66 Szumigalski, A., & Abley, M. (2006). Statement: Reinventing Memory. In *When Earth leaps up* (p. 41). Brick Books.

67 Szumigalski, A. (1997). Afterword. In *On glassy wings* (p. 213). Coteau Books.

68 Szumigalski, A. (1990). The Bigs and The Littles. In *The word, the voice, the text: The life of a writer* (p. 83). Fifth House.

69 Szumigalski, A. (1990). On Getting Things Together. In *The word, the voice, the text: The life of a writer* (p. 122). Fifth House.

CONTRIBUTORS' COMMENTARY AND BIOGRAPHIES

HOLLIE ADAMS is from Windsor, Ontario. She is the author of *Things You've Inherited from Your Mother* (NeWest Press, 2015) and the chapbook *Deliver Me from Swedish Furniture* (Zed Press, 2017), a finalist for the bpNichol Chapbook Award. Her poetry has appeared in *Room*, *The New Quarterly*, *The Malahat Review*, *Contemporary Verse 2*, and elsewhere. Adams teaches at the University of Maine.

Of "Five Days a Week," Adams writes, "I wanted to write a poem that was, to my mind, an elegy for my figure skating career. I was never going to make it to the national or even provincial level (for one thing, I am the most inflexible person I know), but for a third of my life, well into my teenage years, I was very serious about figure skating, practicing five days a week. I sacrificed a lot for the sport, and it gave me a lot in return (some good, some not so good). I think the saddest thing about being a figure skater is that when you give it up, you pretty much give it up for good—it's not like there are adult figure skating beer leagues (though maybe there should be). There just aren't many opportunities to keep doing double lutz jumps recreationally, and the other thing is that your body loses that ability incredibly quickly. So this poem is for all the retired figure skaters who miss their sport and the magic tricks their bodies could once do."

GEORGE AMABILE lives in Winnipeg. He has published twelve books, won many prizes and awards, and had work in over a hundred publications, including *The New Yorker, Harper's, Poetry Magazine, American Poetry Review, Botteghe Oscure,* the *Globe and Mail, The Penguin Book of Canadian Verse, Saturday Night, Poetry Australia, Sur* (Buenos Aires)*, Poetry Canada Review,* and *Canadian Literature.*

Of "Coming of age on my 84th birthday," Amabile writes, "I wrote the first draft seven or eight years ago in a great rush of intense attention. I thought it was good, but the next day it seemed shapeless, vague, tangled up in its own sound effects. I made a few changes, but couldn't get it to 'go,' as a well-known poet whose name I don't remember once put it. So I filed it away and forgot it. Years later, I was looking through my slag heap of failures and, when I read it again, I felt the original impulse clarify and take on new energy. It suddenly started finding new words, and I did the revision in a few hours, much quicker than my usual weeks or months. As I understood what the poem was saying, I added the first stanza. I corrected the mistaken quotation from Whitman and rewrote the rest, changing the phrasing and rearranging the lines so the line ends made poetic sense. I kept the sunset image, but the rain image was new. It refers to something I read somewhere by a Zen master who said awakening could make itself known in something simple, like a new way of hearing rain on the roof."

ERIN BEDFORD lives near Lake Ontario's north shore. In 2018, she was lucky to be mentored by poet Betsy Warland through the Vancouver Manuscript Intensive. Her short work has appeared in *The /tƐmz/ Review*, *Juniper*, *Map Literary*, *Train*, GUEST, *Catamaran Literary Reader*, EVENT, and *The Fiddlehead*. She is the founder and editor of *Pinhole Poetry*, a digital journal and chapbook press.

Of "For my dad who never read my poems but died with a well-thumbed copy of *Watership Down*," Bedford writes, "My dad didn't read much beyond the newspaper during his life, and never got around to reading my poems and novels. He was always supportive of me, though, if not my work specifically. This poem is part of a series of erasures of texts that I know he read, and creating these poems was a way to communicate my grief in a manner that made me feel connected to him."

BILLY-RAY BELCOURT is from the Driftpile Cree Nation in northwest Alberta. He is an assistant professor in the School of Creative Writing at the University of British Columbia. He is the author of five books, most recently *Coexistence: Stories* (Hamish Hamilton, 2024).

Belcourt writes, "I wrote 'According to the CBC ...' in the middle of one of the COVID-19 lockdowns. The CBC released an article documenting that Indigenous peoples were more likely to experience severe forms of illness from the virus than other Canadians. This further compounded our statistical likelihood to die prematurely (as a symptom of colonialism). I felt compelled to write a poetic response; what emerged was my attempt to grieve the loss of the years I won't be able to live, the years my kin have already lost. I couldn't help but register my longing for a country that doesn't generate the conditions in which we die sooner than we should."

BERTRAND BICKERSTETH lives in Moh'kins'tsis (Calgary) in Treaty Seven. He is the author of *The Response of Weeds* (NeWest Press, 2020), which was the recipient of multiple awards, including the Gerald Lampert Memorial Award and the Stephan G. Stephansson Award for Poetry. He currently teaches at Olds College and is writing a collection of poems on Black cowboys.

Of "A Poem about Blackboy's Horse," Bickersteth writes, "After suffering from a year-long bout of writer's block—brought on by the murder of George Floyd in the summer of 2020—I eventually found my way back to writing through the topic of Black cowboys. I was struck by how iconic cowboys are to the west and yet how unknown the existence of Black cowboys is (yes, Black cowboys *here* in Canada). I began writing a series of poems fleshing out their histories and, for some reason, I became obsessed with the moment of death in one of their lives. John Ware, the most famous/unknown cowboy in Canada, died tragically, ironically, when his horse tripped and fell on top of him. I was compelled to write poems that repeated this moment from different vantages. I think knowing that our national awareness of Black cowboys was doomed to die, I wanted to hold on to him as long as I could, stubbornly pause everything in the moment before the end, desperately cling to that moment when his Black life still mattered."

ELISABETH BLAIR is a writer, editor, and multidisciplinary artist based in Anemki Wequedong (Thunder Bay). She's published two chapbooks and a poetry memoir, *because God loves the wasp* (Unsolicited Press, 2022), about the abusive "troubled teen" industry. Advocacy for older adults is at the heart of much of her creative work.

Of "a hunt's surviving duck," Blair writes, "This poem comes from a longer manuscript—a poetry novel that traces the tumultuous, courageous, and passionate life of a nonspeaking one-hundred-year-old woman living in a care facility. She's a mystery to those around her; no one knows who she is or what her life has been like—but the reader gets a special view into her past. In this scene, she's barely twenty years old, and has just left an abusive partner. She's found a way to make ends meet, but she's still on high alert because of the traumas she's endured."

RONNA BLOOM lives in Toronto/Tkaronto. She is the author of seven books of poetry, most recently *A Possible Trust: The Poetry of Ronna Bloom, selected with an introduction by Phil Hall* (Wilfrid Laurier University Press, 2023). Her poems and essays have appeared in *Brick, The New Quarterly, The Lion's Roar*, and elsewhere. *In a Riptide* will be out with Brick Books in 2025.

Bloom writes, "'Where I've Been' was written while I was waiting for a date for surgery. The writing has in it all the high-pitched anxieties of waiting, going, doing, doing nothing, fearing, plus the wider awareness of a meditation practice that (thankfully) entered and carried the poem."

ALISON BRAID-FERNANDEZ is a writer from the Okanagan now living in London, England. She is the author of the chapbook *Little Hunches* (Anstruther Press, 2020.) Her poetry and prose have been published in *Massachusetts Review, EVENT, West Branch, The New Quarterly, Grain,* and elsewhere.

Of "Light Upon the Body," Braid-Fernandez writes, "This

poem came together as a culmination of influences: a painting, a trip with my mother, a song, and a book. At the time of writing, I had been experiencing chronic pain with no diagnosis. The intense feelings of my body seemed at odds with the way I had been putting it down on the page. Pablo Neruda once wrote, 'Arthritis in both ankles!' The poet Jane Hirshfield uses this line in the ending to 'Notebook,' a poem from her book *Ledger*: '"Arthritis in both ankles!" / Neruda wrote in a notebook, / January 3, 1959, on a boat leaving Valparaíso for Venezuela, / limping like an old race horse, then starting his poem.' Our bodies, as the mime Jacques Lecoq says in *The Moving Body*, are sites for transformation and meaning-making. The notes I made about my body tried and failed to describe the pain I felt. I pushed against that inability until I understood I was narrowing an experience that demanded a more fragmented and imaginative complexity."

ROBERT BRINGHURST lives on the British Columbia coast. He is an officer of the Order of Canada. His *Selected Poems* (2009) is published in Canada by Gaspereau Press, in the UK by Jonathan Cape, and in the US by Copper Canyon Press. "Life Poem" appears in his recent book *The Ridge* (Harbour, 2023).

Of "Life Poem," Bringhurst writes, "Stan Dragland—a brilliant critic, teacher, and editor, and an exemplary human being—was one of the best friends Canadian literature ever had. He was my friend too. He did not need a lesson on the nature of language. Still less did he need to be reminded of the perils of bad ecological behaviour. Those just happen to be among the things I am always thinking about—and so they are things I was thinking about when he died."

EMILY CANN has been writing her way back to Epekwitk/PEI ever since she left. She holds an MS in Narrative Medicine from Columbia University, an MA in English Literature from the University of Guelph, and an MFA in Creative Writing from UBC. Her writing has appeared in *carte blanche*, *yolk*, and *FreeFall*. She is currently pursuing Killam-funded doctoral work at Dalhousie University.

Cann writes, "The bizarre confluence of three events precipitated 'The Fox': the long, seemingly endless pandemic years, the disturbing overturning of Roe v. Wade in the US, and the mysterious discovery of a decaying fox carcass beneath my parents' deck. I think this context is legible as the poem attempts to make sense of feelings of loneliness, desire, disgust, and grief in its attendance to the body and the space that the body takes up. At the heart of 'The Fox,' I feel, is change—and the confused mix of hope and despair that accompanies any recognition of impermanence."

ANNE CARSON was born in Canada and lives partly in Iceland.

MOLLY CROSS-BLANCHARD is a white and Métis writer and editor living on unceded Musqueam, Squamish, and Tsleil-Waututh territory. Her debut collection of poetry is *Exhibitionist* (Coach House, 2021). She teaches creative writing and Indigenous studies at Kwantlen Polytechnic University.

Of "Here's the thing," Cross-Blanchard writes, "This poem was written as an attempt to make myself feel better about being single, childless, and approaching my thirties—none of which I particularly wanted to be. But I've got a hot boyfriend now, so SORRY, SUCKAS!!! (Hehe, only joking. I cherish the solitude and freedom my twenties have afforded me, and I hope that gratitude emanates from 'Here's the thing.' Be selfish and satisfy your cravings, friends!)"

LORNA CROZIER, born in Saskatchewan, now lives on Vancouver Island where she is a professor emerita at the University of Victoria. An officer of the Order of Canada, she is the recipient of many major awards, including the Governor General's, Raymond Souster, and Pat Lowther. Her latest books are the memoir *Through the Garden: A Love Story (with Cats)* (McClelland & Stewart, 2022) and the poetry collection *After That* (McClelland & Stewart, 2023).

Of "December's End," Crozier writes, "In March 2019, my partner of almost forty years, Patrick Lane, died. When he fell ill three years before his death, I began writing about our life together as poets. The story included the biography of the five cats who had been our companions. One of the main characters was poetry itself. The book came out as *Through the Garden: A Love Story (with Cats)* in 2021. During the final stages of its editing I fell back into poetry as another way of trying to understand the loss of my beloved. Patrick was always a gardener of great insight and passion. When he left, he left me with a beautiful garden, one in which he'd walked every pathway and touched every plant and stone. I looked for him there, and in some ways and at some times, I found him, at least an image of him from the past, tending and nurturing what he loved."

KAYLA CZAGA lives on the traditional territory of the Lekwungen people, the Songhees and Esquimalt Nations. She is the author of three poetry collections, most recently *Midway* (House of Anansi, 2024.)

Czaga writes, "'Safe Despair' was inspired by a recent rereading of Emily Dickinson's poetry. The title is taken from the poem that begins: 'Safe Despair it is that raves— / Agony is frugal,' and the poem's concept sprang from a more famous poem, 'Because I could not stop for Death.' Rereading that line, I wondered why a speaker might not be able to stop for Death. One reason I came up with: maybe she doesn't want to. Which led to the question, why doesn't she want to stop? Well... maybe she's angry? Why? Are they lovers? Ex-lovers? Then I remembered a scene from a television show: the girlfriend is so mad at her boyfriend that she refuses to get in his car and walks alongside while he drives next to her, demanding she get in. Could 'kindly,' in this situation, be taken ironically? The poem unfolded from there. I often use reading as a springboard for writing, asking myself sort of literal, sometimes beside-the-point, questions about a poem I like or struggle with. In the case of 'Safe Despair,' some of the source material stayed in the poem."

EVELYNA EKOKO-KAY is a writer and activist from Hamilton, Ontario. She holds an MFA in poetry from the University of Guelph. Her writing has been featured in *The Ex-Puritan*, *Midnight Sun Magazine*, Biblioasis' *Best Canadian Poetry 2023* (2022), and Book*hug's *Write Across Canada: An Anthology of Emerging Writers* (2019). She lives with her fiancée, Rachel, and their three beautiful, terrible cats.

Of "on my shoulders," Ekoko-Kay writes, "According to a 2017 paper in *Nature*, allistic (non-autistic) people can identify within milliseconds of meeting an autistic person that something is different and determine that they have less interest in socializing with them than with allistic peers. These biases disappear when engaging with an autistic person solely through text but emerge in allistics even when looking at a photograph of an autistic person, indicating that it is not our actual words or 'social skills' that are the 'problem' but our bodies. These 'thin-slice judgments' are instinctive, and therefore difficult to challenge. 'On my shoulders' reflects my embodied experience as an autistic person. Written after a disastrous two-month stint as a restaurant hostess, the poem grapples with the experience of social exclusion as a physical phenomenon. My body does not respond to the requests I make of it, and often my body is responded to socially as a source of discomfort, difficulty, and deficiency. In writing and sharing this poem, I hope to challenge allistic neurotypicals to examine their instinctive reactions; to peel apart the paperthin pieces of perception and examine each with care."

KATE GENEVIEVE is a writer born and raised in Vancouver. She is a graduate of the University of Edinburgh, where she received a master's degree in creative writing. Her poems have appeared in *carte blanche*, *The Malahat Review*, *Best Canadian Poetry*, and are forthcoming in *The Mid-American Review* and *Queen's Quarterly*.

Of "Wheels on the Bus Go," Genevieve writes, "I wrote this poem while living in Edinburgh and after receiving news of yet another school shooting in the United States involving young children. This poem came from a place of anger and helplessness in the wake of yet another tragedy at the hands of a gunman, and from a place of incredulity that this continues to happen again and again. The poem is a stark, somewhat surreal piece in which the victims are retrieved, brought home and, like their friends, are subject to the same unimaginable dangers each and every day. I wanted the piece to feel endless and somewhat routined, drawing attention to the repetitive tasks that take place each day, highlighting the absurdity of life moving ahead amidst such devastation while also underscoring the recurrent nature of those same, preventable tragedies. I was compelled to create a juxtaposition between the innocent, colourful, and cozy elements of childhood and the inhumane nature of such atrocities."

SUSAN GILLIS has lived on the east and west coasts of Canada and now makes her home in rural Ontario, on traditional Omàmìwininì (Algonquin) territory. She has published four books of poetry, most recently *Yellow Crane* (Brick, 2018), and is a member of the collaborative group Yoko's Dogs.

Of "Come In, Come In," Gillis writes, "From the small observed detail of autumn leaves seeming to fall upwards, the poem gathered energy and form through associations: a set of possible (or impossible?) answers, maybe, to probable (or improbable?) questions randomly posed. Or if not quite random, then generated through the back-and-forth of memory and impression. When the water, or the surface of it, spoke out with the invitation to dive in, I figured this draft was intent on becoming a poem."

SUE GOYETTE lives in K'jipuktuk (Halifax) and has published nine books of poems and a novel. Her latest collections are *Monoculture* (Gaspereau Press, 2022) and *A Different Species of Breathing: The Poetry of Sue Goyette,* edited by Bart Vautour (Wilfrid Laurier University Press, 2023). Sue teaches in the creative writing program at Dalhousie University.

Goyette writes, "My longing for my mother was active and alert soon after she died. I wrote 'surprise: an armoire (in a sunny spot, I'm hoping)' in those early days when I was keen for her company, parched, and on the lookout for any sign of her: sassy cardinals, full-throated lilies, a slant of light that stopped on her photograph. I was reassembling into understanding what the long haul without her would be like. There was something about how this armoire was being carried from the truck to a neighbour's house, almost tenderly, that moved me, and I felt that longing and a hope that her spirit/energy was being carried with the same care, which sounds a little intense, dramatic even, and strange outside of the moment I was in, but in the galactic moments grieving brings, there she was, hopefully heading to the kind of sunny spot she used to love basking in."

CATHERINE GRAHAM, a writer from Ontario, has published seven poetry books and two novels. *Æther: An Out-of-Body Lyric* (Wolsak & Wynn, 2021) was a finalist for the Trillium Book Award and the Toronto Book Award, and won the Fred Kerner Book Award. *Put Flowers Around Us and Pretend We're Dead: New and Selected Poems* (Wolsak & Wynn, 2023) is her latest book. www.catherinegraham.com

Of "Last Shadow," Graham writes, "I am fortunate to have lines of poetry appear in my dreams. These are scribbled in a bedside notebook, and if I can decipher the writing, provide much raw material for my current poems. I use them as strands to uncover the poetic logic as I follow the undercurrent of emotion, voice, tone and story. Some of these dream lines worked their way into my poem 'Last Shadow.' I remain forever hopeful that one day I will actually have a dream in which I can fly."

HENRY HEAVYSHIELD is a Blackfoot reader and writer from Kainai (Blood Tribe First Nation) living at home on Treaty #7 territory. His work has appeared in several Canadian literary magazines and journals, including *Riddle Fence* (2023 poetry contest winner) and *The Capilano Review* (2023 contest winner). He was also a 2024 Bronwen Wallace Award finalist in the short fiction category.

Of "My Brother, *Om'ahkokota* (gopher)," Heavyshield writes, "Richardson's ground squirrel, *Urocitellus richardsonii*, gophers. Or, for *siksikaitsitapi* (Blackfoot), we know them as *om'ahkokota* (lit. 'big snared one'). If you're from the Prairies you will be familiar with their daredevil behaviour crossing roads and highways. I wanted to write a mythology that accounted for this phenomenon. This poem was from an unpublished chapbook titled *The Moon of Finding My Way Home*, a series of narrative poems about metempsychosis. The speaker's soul inhabits the bodies of animals, including a trout, stellar jay, moose, black fly, funnel-web spider, and gopher before finally reaching his lover's bed. In line with Blackfoot narrative traditions, animal and plant relations feature prominently in my work. The original poem was about grieving the death of my late cousin-brother, Justin Healy, whom we lost the previous summer. I rewrote the ending, however, because I wanted the story to focus on courage and tension rather than loss. Suspense is a close relative to hope. I would like to thank guest editor Brandi Bird for giving my poem a home in *The Ex-Puritan's* special Indigenous Storytelling issue. Finally, I would like to thank the continued support of my family and community. *nitsíniiyi'taki* (thank you)."

GERALD HILL, of Regina, Saskatchewan, has published seven poetry collections, most recently *Crooked at the Far End* (Radiant Press, 2020). He was poet laureate of Saskatchewan in 2016.

Oak Floors!, his musical, was produced by All-Terrain Theatre in Regina in 2023.

Of "To Celebrate Waves Right to Left in a Shirt-Rippling Wind, Tavira, Portugal," Hill writes, "The poem, set on a sandy island just off Tavira, Portugal, celebrates the all-encompassing natural sensations of a timeless moment during my travels through Andalusia in 2014. The poem also reminds us, or me at least, that any such moment is a matter of language as much as natural sensation. Language translates emotion; language creates what we feel."

ALEXANDER HOLLENBERG is from Hamilton, Ontario. He is a Pushcart-nominated poet and professor of storytelling who loves to write about crows and fish. Some of his new work can be found in *Arc Poetry Magazine, The New Quarterly, Prairie Fire,* and *Grain.* Recently, he won *Contemporary Verse 2*'s Two-Day Poem Contest and was shortlisted for the Nick Blatchford Occasional Verse Contest. His debut collection, *Human Story will not Consume the Cosmos*, will be published by Gaspereau in 2025.

Hollenberg writes, "I wrote 'origin story, with crow' for *Contemporary Verse 2*'s Two-Day Poem Contest. They gave us ten compulsory words and forty-eight hours. Maybe it was because it forced me to block out from my schedule an entire sunny weekend in April to just write, or maybe it was because I was compelled—with no time for self-doubt—to learn and use some fantastically complex new words (abyssalpelagic! syzygy!), but it was—surprisingly—one of the most delightful writing experiences I've had in a long time. I'm fascinated by origin stories, their particular power to shape our values by staking their claims as beginnings, and then the strange alchemical audacity that in those beginnings are the seeds of our ends. In the midst of our

Anthropocene moment, in the midst of so much catastrophe, this poem was an attempt to see what a beginning might look like if it were a little less audacious, a little less human."

KIM JUNE JOHNSON lives on Vancouver Island on the unceded traditional territory of the K'ómoks First Nation with her teen daughter. Her poems and essays have appeared in *Prairie Fire, The New Quarterly, FOLKLIFE,* and elsewhere. She hosts an online mindful-writing community called "Cozy Sunday Write-Ins" and works as a religious trauma coach at healingground.ca.

Of "I Don't Know What to Do about the World," Johnson writes, "I have a regular writing practice, and this poem came on a morning in early July 2021 when Lytton, BC, was being ravaged by wildfire and the Indigenous children's remains had recently been found near the site of Kamloops Indian Residential School. That morning, when I sat down to write at my picnic table, the world had a wrecked feel to it. The robin appeared midway through the poem, so I wove it in. The poem in its current form is very close to the way it came onto the page. One of my favourite poets, Marie Howe, says that art helps us to let our hearts break open rather than close. I do tend to turn to poem-writing when I find myself at this crossroads."

EVE JOSEPH lives in Victoria and works on the unceded territory of the Lekwungen people. Her three books of poetry were nominated for the Dorothy Livesay Award. *In the Slender Margin* won the Hubert Evans nonfiction award. *Quarrels* won the 2019 Griffin Prize.

Of "superpowers," Joseph writes, "I wrote this poem in a friend's cottage at Robert's Creek. I remember looking at the clouds moving over the water and wondering idly what they would do without wind. I had been 'trying to find' the poem for a few days and the first few lines about not looking came out of that. What would happen if, instead of looking for the poem, I turned away from it? The lines came quickly after that until the end, at which point I felt myself turn to craft to try and write an ending. Even in the poem I knew that was a mistake…so I wrote that down and used the metaphor of the clouds and wind to show how the gift of the poem can get weighted down by craft."

EVELYN LAU is a lifelong Vancouverite who has published fourteen books, including nine volumes of poetry. Her poetry has received the Milton Acorn Award, the Pat Lowther Award, and a National Magazine Award. From 2011–2014, Evelyn served as Vancouver's poet laureate. Her latest collection, *Cactus Gardens* (Anvil, 2022), received the Fred Cogswell Award.

Of "Mindful," Lau writes, "Despite all the wonders of the west coast, its grey and gloomy winters are challenging for those of us prone to depression. 'Mindful' is an attempt to call attention to the startling moments of beauty that exist in the rain and the dark. I wrote the poem for a friend who was learning how to conduct a traditional tea ceremony as part of his attempt to slow down and be more mindful; he had begun amassing an impressive tea collection, and spoke of tasting notes the way a sommelier might speak about wine—hence, my cheeky reference to the taste of 'snow leopard.'"

Y. S. LEE lives in Kingston, Ontario. She is the author of a poetry chapbook, *Exit Permit* (Anstruther Press, 2023), and a winner of *Contemporary Verse 2*'s Foster Poetry Prize. Her fiction includes the award-winning YA mystery series The Agency (Candlewick Press) and a forthcoming picture book, *Mrs. Nobody* (Groundwood Books).

Lee writes, "I wrote 'He/him' for my high-school bestie when he came out as a trans man. I was thrilled for him and wanted to celebrate his identity. Gender transition is sometimes seen as slow and arduous, but I also want to keep sight of what a triumph it is. Plus, he and I did our share of impulsive stuff as teens and I'm interested in how even dumbass near-disasters can offer moments of insight, if we pay attention."

D. A. LOCKHART resides at the south shore of Waawiiyaatanong, in the lands currently held by Windsor, Ontario. His recent work includes *North of Middle Island* (Kegedonce, 2023) and *Bearmen Descend Upon Gimli* (Frontenac House, 2021). Lockhart is a graduate of the Indiana University–Bloomington MFA in Creative Writing program. He is pùkuwànkoamimëns of the Eelünaapéewi Lahkéewiit (Moravian of the Thames First Nation).

Of "Hussain Recites Ginsberg While Driving Down Kedzie," Lockhart writes, "A couple of autumns back, I was in Chicago to deliver an Indigenous Peoples Day talk at Lake Forest College along with visiting a dear friend. This piece arises during that visit and particularly during a trip home after a shared reading near Logan Square. Myself and fellow poet Benjamin Goluboff used a rideshare to get back to his place. We, of course, called our clans and relations (myself Lenape and Ben being Jewish American) upon settling into the shared ride. The driver's name was Hussain and he was a Palestinian immigrant who'd come to the area a good number of years back. Both Hussain and my fellow poet were proud Chicagoans and recited a shared love of the place. At an idle point in the conversation, we came to what we do for a living and when we revealed we were poets, Hussain immediately launched into a recitation of Ginsberg's "Howl." He had turned down the radio. And his recitation became a soundtrack for the night street-scapes of Chicago as we crawled our way through traffic."

FAREH MALIK is a writer and spoken word artist who is based in the Greater Toronto Area. He was the winner of the 2023 Austin Clarke Prize in Literary Excellence and the 2022 RBC PEN Canada New Voices Award. Fareh is the author of *Streams that Lead Somewhere* (Mawenzi House, 2022), which received the 2023 Hamilton Literary Award in Poetry.

Of "Praise Us, for We Are Dead," Malik writes, "I turned thirty this year. To be honest, I think there was a time that I never imagined myself getting to this age. The more I hear of my people around the world, the more I realize how much of a privilege it is to grow older. My birthday was on a Friday, and as my sweat dropped onto the janamaz at Jummah prayer, it reminded me of an image I saw of a bullet-hole-riddled prayer mat in Gaza. That was also what inspired the form of the poem. This poem is an exploration of the tangled parts that live within our bodies and souls. I wrote it as an avenue of unravelling: an unravelling of generational curses, an unravelling of displacement, and an unravelling of hurt that is felt through the diameter of the Earth."

DAVID MARTIN lives in Calgary, where he works as a literacy instructor and as an organizer for the Single Onion Poetry Series. He is the author of *Tar Swan* (NeWest Press, 2018), *Kink Bands* (NeWest Press, 2023), and *Limited Verse* (University of Calgary Press, 2024).

Of "Tinnitus," Martin writes, "I've lived with tinnitus as a left-ear companion for about twenty-five years. Most days I don't notice it much, but sometimes the ringing can become obtrusive. The poem uses a number of musical terms to describe the condition and how I relate to it. In music, a pedal point is a sustained tone that other pitches sound against, sometimes in harmony and sometimes with dissonance. A tonic, again in music theory, is the first note in a musical scale, which acts as the home base or resolution point. My advice is to wear earplugs when attending a loud concert!"

DOMENICA MARTINELLO lives in Montreal. She is the author of two books of poetry, *Good Want* (Coach House, 2024) and *All Day I Dream about Sirens* (Coach House, 2019). The eponymous poem from *Good Want* won the *Malahat Review*'s Long Poem Prize in 2023.

Of "Infinity Mirror," Martinello writes, "I'd been considering how intergenerational trauma forms bonds across matriarchal lineages. It links grandmothers, mothers, and daughters in an ongoing cycle in which, like a chemical reaction, birth reconfigures and transforms the roles: daughter into mother, mother into grandmother, and so on, an endless series of reflections. While considering this, I learned the astounding fact that women are born with all the eggs they'll ever carry, which creates an additional layer of biological continuity. My point of origin was as a cell inside my mother, who was a fetus inside my grandmother, alongside the fetus of her twin, my aunt, who had the cells of my cousins within her—all these shared points of latent possibility inside the nexus of one complicated woman. It's also, spiritually, a little claustrophobic. The poem is a portrait of this complicated woman, the grandmother, reflected in an infinity mirror, but resisting the illusion of depth that such a mirror creates."

CASSIDY MCFADZEAN was born in Regina, studied poetry at the Iowa Writers' Workshop and fiction at Brooklyn College, and currently lives in Toronto. She is the author of three books of poetry, most recently *Crying Dress* (House of Anansi, 2024).

McFadzean writes, "I wrote 'Storm King' after visiting Storm King Art Center in New York's Hudson Valley. I wanted to capture the strangeness of walking around these massive sculptures, imagining them as offerings to a powerful, magical entity. The poem makes specific mention of Maya Lin's *Storm King Wavefield* (2007–08). At the time, the *Wavefield* was sadly closed, but I've since returned, and the feeling of running over the waves was exhilarating, unlocking a child-like joy absent in this particular poem."

CARMELITA MCGRATH is from rural Newfoundland and currently lives in St. John's. She is an author of poetry, fiction and children's literature who also works as an editor. Her poetry collections include the award-winning *Escape Velocity* (icehouse poetry/Goose Lane Editions, 2013) and *To the New World* (Killick Press, 1997).

Of "Visit, July 25, 2020," McGrath writes, "I wrote this poem during my first 'plague summer,' which would be followed by more plague seasons. After living in Montreal for several years, I found myself homeless and without paying work. To survive, I moved through a number of temporary living situations, including the chaotic one featured here. I hope sweet G. made it. Along the way, I encountered many situations of dislocation, turmoil, and hope. My journals from that time form the basis of my new poetry collection-in-progress."

ERÍN MOURE is a Montreal poet and translator of poetry. Her most recent book is *Theophylline: An Aporetic Migration via the modernisms of Rukeyser, Bishop, Grimké* (House of Anansi, 2023), and most recent translations are Chantal Neveu's *you* into English from French (Book*hug Press, 2024) and Chus Pato's *Chair de Léviathan* into French from Galician (Éditions Apic, 2024).

Moure writes, "In 'The Straying of All Translation: A Phrase Archive' I struggled with the trembling problematic of translating a Galician sentence in a work by Chus Pato (a sentence she had approximated into her Galician from the French of Jean-Luc Nancy) into English. In the same way that a person grabs at any bit of paper to scribble something down, I was writing out my struggle as an email to myself. Do I follow the professional norm and translate the phrase from French, not from her Galician? Or do I translate it from Pato's Galician and get even further from the French? The phrase itself is very difficult to translate in isolation, as it gains its meaning from the sentences in French that precede and follow it, which are not in the Pato piece I am translating! Nancy's original French is a wordplay with *found* (to begin something, like a dynasty) and *found* (as in smelt, melt down, dissolve) and *founder* (flop and fail). Pato skips this wordplay in Galician but I wanted to capture it in my English version of her text. You can see what I did here: www.berfrois.com/2022/09/chus-patos-letter-to-europe. And my email became this polyglot image-poem."

TOLU OLORUNTOBA is a poet, project management person, and lapsed physician from Ibadan, Nigeria. He is the author of

The Junta of Happenstance (Palimpsest Press, 2021) and *Each One a Furnace* (McClelland & Stewart, 2022). His work has won the Griffin Poetry Prize and Governor General's Literary Award for Poetry in English. He lives in Calgary, Alberta, with his family.

On "'Understand me, love me, answer me': 77 Questions from Anne Szumigalski," Oloruntoba writes, "In 2021, I was invited by the League of Canadian Poets to deliver the twentieth-anniversary Anne Szumigalski Lecture. Prompted by a review written by the poet Samantha Jones, I had been ruminating on the role questions play in the divination of the human condition. In that second year of the COVID-19 pandemic, questions (many still unanswered) abounded. Existential, practical, metaphysical, biological . . . there was no end to them. As I examined Anne Szumigalski's oeuvre to find an insight that could honour her legacy, I was drawn to the impressive number and range of questions her poems asked. My cento collages seventy-seven of those questions (one for each of Szimigalski's years) from the following titles: *Dogstones: Selected and New Poems*, *On Glassy Wings: Poems New & Selected*, *A Peeled Wand*, *The Word, The Voice, The Text: The Life of a Writer*, and *When Earth Leaps Up*. On the ethos and ethics of centos: they have persisted since at least Homer and Virgil. The recombination and sampling evident in oral traditions also suggest that the approach has persisted from even earlier times. A cento offers a zoomed-in version of the creative process, in which an artist takes elements from a variety of sources, combines them with perspective, imbues them with direction, and, combining them with arcane elements, creates a new object. At the intersection of these two concepts is an idea: Could we curate our questions, plot their slope, perhaps, and thus derive the saving answers we need?"

CATHERINE OWEN, from Vancouver, is the author of sixteen collections of poetry and prose. Her most recent title is *Moving to Delilah* (Freehand Books, 2024). She reviews, edits, and hosts the podcast *Ms. Lyric's Poetry Outlaws* from her 1905 home in Edmonton.

Of "Fall," Owen writes, "I've been writing 'weather says' poems for a few years now for my ever-shifting manuscript *Commemorations by the Weather*. I like to imagine the weather has a voice as Louise Glück did with flowers, occasionally praising with their iterations, but more often condemning the stupidities of humanity as we fail to negotiate the massive interruptions we've created in natural cycles, mostly through insane over-consumption. So, in this poem the weather is speaking of normalizations of chaos throughout myth and history. And of how we are now playing a terrifying game of effectively tossing the 'hot potato' of our actions about, suffering the consequences and, far too often, carrying on with our dangerous play anyway."

MOLLY PEACOCK lives in Toronto and has published eight books of poems, including *The Widow's Crayon Box* (W. W. Norton, 2024). She inaugurated *The Best Canadian Poetry* series in 2008 with Tightrope Books, editing it until 2017, and is delighted to return as a contributor. Peacock is also the author of two biographies of women artists, *The Paper Garden* (Emblem Editions, 2011) and *Flower Diary* (ECW Press, 2021), and the memoir *Paradise, Piece by Piece* (Riverhead, 1998).

Of "Honey Crisp," Peacock writes, "After my husband died, I cried for twenty-eight days straight. On the twenty-ninth day, I woke without tears, picked up a blue mechanical pencil, and began to write the poems that would become *The Widow's Crayon Box*.

'Honey Crisp' literally began when I walked to the refrigerator. There was my husband's last apple—I couldn't throw it out. In the back of my mind was William Blake, who spoke to a Tyger. Could I write a poem where I spoke to the apple, telling it what happened to my husband, reminding it of its origins, how I bought it, and why it would never be eaten? That idea could go very, very wrong! But widowhood made me fearless. I pulled out a purple pad (what other colour do widows use?) and drafted the poem. It amazed me that if I was simple and direct, like a seventeenth-century poet talking to an animal, I could infuse the poem with all I felt. P.S. The apple stayed in the fridge after the poem. I painted a watercolour of it. Then put it back. A long time after that, I buried the almost-dried apple with the geraniums in my balcony garden."

MIRANDA PEARSON is originally from England but lived in Vancouver for many years. She is the author of six books of poetry, most recently *Bridestones* (McGill–Queen's University Press, 2024). Previous titles *Harbour* (Oolican, 2009) and *The Fire Extinguisher* (Oolichan, 2015) were both finalists for the Dorothy Livesay BC Book Prize. Miranda has taught creative writing at Simon Fraser University and at the University of British Columbia, worked as a psychiatric nurse, and currently writes, walks, swims, and makes visual art.

Of "Bridestones," Pearson writes, "The Bridestones are a group of millstone-grit rocks and boulders near Todmorden, West Yorkshire. I went there with a friend and was transported by their stark beauty and scale. She told me that Ted Hughes (who had lived nearby) wrote a poem also titled 'Bridestones,' and I use a quote from it as an epigraph to mine—a women's reply/response. 'You do nothing casual here' sets the poem up as serious, though in fact the poem moves between solemn and breezy, contrasting the weight and age of the rocks with the joyful life-force of the birds. The friend I visited the stones with is a woman I loved—was *in* love with—when I was nineteen. We lost touch for forty years and had recently reunited and were able to build a new and wiser friendship. It was a gift to be able to do that. So as well as being about that extraordinary place in Yorkshire, 'Bridestones' is about the durability and timelessness of love. One interesting note is that I had to pay the Ted Hughes Foundation £150 for permission to use those five words 'you do nothing casual here.' However, I have used this particular poem as the overall title of my latest book, so I think it was worth it."

PAULINE PETERS is a queer African Canadian writer living in Toronto, the territory of the Mississaugas of the Credit, the Anishnabeg, the Chippewa, the Haudenosaunee and the Wendat peoples. Her poetry has been published in *Canadian Literature*, *The Fiddlehead*, PRISM *international*, and *The Malahat Review* among others. Her chapbook, *The Salted Woman*, was published in Britain by Hedgespoken Press.

Of "Housebreaking," Peters writes, "Sometimes I'm lucky and I write a poem that calms me down. I am a lot more anxious than I may appear. I write a lot about spirituality and mythology. This poem is a continuation of a theme I've been exploring and revisiting for a long time, the idea of the feminine divine. I focus on the feminine divine to redress an imbalance: I feel that the image and qualities of the male divine need to be balanced and tempered. What's unusual for me in this poem is that it is written in the first person and the woman is an ordinary person become large, become divine. This poem also addresses another recurring theme for me, which is our relationship with the earth. I return to this theme often and investigate it as much as I can. The turtle motif is also a recurring one. Turtles play a big part in my world."

AMANDA PROCTOR is a writer from South Slocan, British Columbia, the unceded territory of the Ktunaxa, Sinixt, Secwepemc, and Syilx Nations. She is an MFA candidate in creative writing at the University of Guelph and holds a BA from the University of Victoria. Her work has appeared in *Room, Arc Poetry Magazine, The Antigonish Review, Prairie Fire, Augur,* and elsewhere.

Of "I found a place where time stands still," Proctor writes, "I wrote this poem after reading Carlo Rovelli's book *The Order of Time,* where I found its epigraph. That line opened a new way of considering time for me, in which the past and the future could be just as alive as the present. While I was reading, I found myself thinking about my grandmother, a Belarusian survivor of forced labour, displacement, and familial separation during the Second World War. A family member had recently told me that, as the German army invaded Mayzr, Belarus, where my grandmother worked, she fled fifty kilometers through the forest to Potashnya, where her family lived. I wrote this poem as I tried to process this story, hoping to hold on to some of the complexity of my grandmother's life, not just the horror she experienced during the war, but the tenderness of our relationship, her ability as a gardener, and her resilience. The writing process allowed me to intertwine our narratives, creating a simultaneity of our experiences that could be alive in the present, if only in this poem."

SHANNON QUINN lives in Toronto, Dish with One Spoon Territory. She is the author of three collections of poetry, her most recent being *Mouthful of Bees* (Mansfield Press, 2022). Quinn's work has been published in *Arc Poetry Magazine, The Malahat Review, Contemporary Verse 2, Grain, Prairie Fire, Geez,* and *subTerrain.* She is also the author of the chapbook *Wonderbeast* (Anstruther Press, 2023).

Of "Feral," Quinn writes, "I was interested in exploring acts of everyday divinity and what we call upon to quell fear. I'm trying to invite in some of the small acts of resilience that allow us fragile points of connection. My hope in this piece is that we all have a moment of *flagrant grace turned wild with wonder* and that we carry it forward, in learning to treasure each other."

ARMAND GARNET RUFFO is the recipient of a Life Member award from the League of Canadian Poets and the Latner Canada Writers' Trust Poetry Prize. He is considered a major contributor to both Indigenous literature and Indigenous literary scholarship in Canada. His latest publication is *The Dialogues: The Song of Francis Pegahmagabow* (Wolsak & Wynn, 2024). He teaches at Queen's University and lives in Kingston.

Of "Resting II," Ruffo writes, "I was raised in a remote northern town that had a residential school. Chapleau's original St. John's Anglican Residential School ran from 1907 to 1919, and a second, bigger school to accommodate more children ran from 1920 to 1948. An unmarked graveyard consisting of forty-two graves was discovered near the second school between the road and railway tracks leading into the town. A few years ago, while I was visiting family on the Fox Lake Reserve, the community held a ceremony at the site of the discovered burial ground. As I was standing in a circle with smoke from burning sweetgrass wafting through the air, I looked over to where the children were buried, and I noticed some tiny green shoots growing up through the damp leaves that covered the area. I thought of my own son, whom I had tucked into bed nightly. A simple gesture of love that had been taken away from these children. The poem came quickly. It needed to be written."

ANNE SIMPSON lives outside Antigonish in Nova Scotia. She has written five books of poetry and three novels; her most recent collection of poems is *Strange Attractor* (McClelland & Stewart, 2019). An earlier book of poetry, *Loop* (McClelland & Stewart, 2003) was awarded the Griffin Poetry Prize. She has been a writer-in-residence at universities and libraries across the country.

Simpson writes, "'The Golden Boat' is named after a small golden boat, part of the Broighter Hoard, in the National Museum of Ireland. My first attempt at a poem didn't lead anywhere. Then I came across Cy Twombly's cycle of works called *Coronation of Sesostris*. I knew he'd been inspired by the boat from the Broighter Hoard because it has an unmistakable shape. Twombly had found a way of using that magical little boat to reveal his ideas about myth, and voyages, and about the elusive figure of Sesostris. I still didn't have a way into my poem, though I knew the golden boat was part of it. It was only when I found myself thinking about several friends who were in the hospital that things started to take shape. 'The Golden Boat' became a way for me to consider debilitating illness and the passage through it."

CAROLYN SMART lives north of Kingston, Ontario. She is the author of six poetry collections including *Hooked* and *Careen* (both from Brick Books), and an award-winning memoir. She founded the Bronwen Wallace Award for Emerging Writers, and for three decades was the director of creative writing at Queen's University. She mentors and edits emerging writers through her website, www.carolynsmartediting.ca

Smart writes, "'Grip' describes the instability and broken-hearted state I found myself in following my partner's cancer diagnosis and my care for him at home. I sought solace in the books I loved in childhood when everything seemed possible, but even they seemed changed beyond repair. In this poem I express the anger I felt at the terrible situation we found ourselves in, and the small attempts I made to make the days somehow more bearable."

KAREN SOLIE was born in Moose Jaw and grew up in southwest Saskatchewan. Her sixth collection of poetry, *Wellwater*, will be published in 2025.

Of "Flashlight," Solie writes, "As we age, we lose people. The poem considers a recent loss in the light of an older one."

CATHERINE ST. DENIS lives on the unceded territories of the Lekwungen-speaking peoples in Victoria, BC. Her work has appeared in *Rattle*, *The Malahat Review, Grain, Arc Poetry Magazine, Canthius*, and *The Humber Literary Review*. Catherine was a finalist for PEN Canada's New Voices Award in both 2022 and 2023. She is a creative writing MFA candidate at the University of British Columbia.

Of "Five Years After Joe Overdosed on Fentanyl," St. Denis writes, "My daughter lost her father to a fentanyl overdose when she was six years old. Grief has a way of seeding itself into the minutiae of life, sending up shoots at the strangest of times. For me, this happened as I was teaching the *Thriller* dance to my grade seven students five years after Joe's passing. It was the first poem I had written in sixteen years."

OWEN TORREY is a writer from Toronto. His poems have appeared in the *Literary Review of Canada, Canadian Literature, Geist, Maisonneuve, Gulf Coast, The Malahat Review,* and *Oxonian Review,* along with being longlisted for the CBC Poetry Prize and awarded Harvard University's Roger Conant Hatch Prize for Lyric Poetry. Owen is currently an MFA candidate in poetry at Brown University.

Torrey writes, "'CV' is a small shaving cut from a much longer poem that I tried and failed for weeks to shape. I knew it wasn't working; I couldn't find my way out. When I showed a draft to a friend, she suggested that a phrase that came near the end ('Now I'm remembering another / thing') should instead be the poem's opening line. Once I had that in place (bless you, Penny), the rest of the poem—shorter now, more blunt and angled—unfolded from there. It helped me realize that what appears to be a door going out can also always be a door going in—or, as the Czech poet Ivan Wernisch puts it, 'The steps going down / And the steps going up / Are one.' It's something I've tried to remember, in writing and in life, since."

MICHAEL TRUSSLER lives in Treaty 4 Territory in Regina. He has received Saskatchewan Book Awards for poetry, nonfiction and short stories. His memoir concerning mental illness, *The Sunday Book*, was published by Palimpsest Press in 2022. This poem appears in *10:10* (Goose Lane, 2024), a book that specifically engages with what it means to be alive at the beginning of the Anthropocene.

Of "D̶e̶c̶o̶y̶," Trussler writes, "What is the role of the lyric poem at the onset of the Anthropocene? I don't know. I'm skeptical, though, that the conventions of the lyric—intense subjective experience, embodied most often in a singular voice—can grasp the amplitude of what's happening. And yet, lyric thought, especially as explored by Jan Zwicky and Tim Lilburn, can perhaps be a way of articulating something of what it means to be alive at this moment. But to do so in a way that recognizes the non-human summons what perhaps is oldest in the lyric: doubt, conjuring, a kind of self-negating love for the form and the actual. To protect and repudiate simultaneously, almost but not solely through irony."

SARA TRUUVERT is a writer from Ontario. Her poetry and short fiction have appeared in *Ploughshares*, PRISM *international*, the *Chicago Quarterly Review*, *Room Magazine*, *Arc Poetry Magazine*, and elsewhere.

Of "You Grew an Orange," Truuvert writes, "This poem is about my grandpa, who has enough kindness, curiosity, and joie de vivre to inspire thousands of poems. He has an incredible green thumb and did indeed grow an orange from a tiny tree in his apartment."

ROB WINGER lives in the hills northeast of Toronto, where he teaches English and creative writing at Trent University. He is the author of four books of poetry, most recently *It Doesn't Matter What We Meant* (McClelland & Stewart, 2021).

Of "Near Dark Park," Winger writes, "My partner and I were meeting, for dinner, the hosts (two wondrous, friendly, generous strangers) who had put us up for a week-long stay in Marin County, just north of San Francisco. But we were early. So we decided to check out the side streets that meandered up the hills in Larkspur, where tiny pockets of redwood forest remained in place despite all the houses and traffic everywhere. It was January. Many roads had been flooded all that week since California had been receiving what they called an 'atmospheric river,' meaning that the Pacific had been pounding the coast and rain had been overfilling all the drainage ditches. As we turned a corner and drifted past this amazing little kids' park, nicknamed, I later learned, 'dark park,' we saw the tree, right there, growing in a protected bed right in the middle of the road. There was something about the fact of it, there, the tree, that stayed with both of us long after. The poem, I think, tries to talk about why that might be."

JAEYUN YOO is a Korean-Canadian poet and psychiatrist living on the unceded territories of the Musqueam, Squamish, and Tsleil-Waututh peoples, also known as Vancouver. Her poems have appeared in *Room, Contemporary Verse 2, Canthius,* and elsewhere. She is the winner of *The Fiddlehead*'s 2023 Ralph Gustafson Poetry Prize and has been nominated for Best of the Net.

Of "Orchids," Yoo writes, "This poem was born out of a wish for a safe world. I was inspired to write this poem after reading news articles about misogyny and violence against women. I wanted to hold space for narratives of resilience and remembrance, as well as express my heartbreak and rage about the countless traumas and threats that women encounter in society. There is great strength in stories of survival. However, I dream of a future when there is nothing to survive from—when people can be free to live their ordinary and extraordinary lives without fear."

NOTABLE POEMS

Ashleigh A. Allen, "Strangers, then papercuts," *Contemporary Verse 2* 46.1

Chris Banks, "Sonnet," *The Walrus* September/October 2023

Dessa Bayrock, "dessa dips into the water with the molluscs, disappears," *The Peter F. Yacht Club* 31

Ashley-Elizabeth Best, "Side Effects II," *Arc Poetry Magazine* 102

Selina Boan, "The Internet's Advice on How to Survive the Apocalypse Is a Hot Mess\," *Arc Poetry Magazine* 100

Marilyn Bowering, "Emergency," *Grain* 50.4

Kate Cayley, "Blue Houses," *The Fiddlehead* 294

George Elliot Clark, "XXXIV," *Columba Poetry* Winter 2023

Marisa P. Clark, "Female Lesser Goldfinch, I," *Prairie Fire* 44.1

Jan Conn, "Late Summer," *The Fiddlehead* 295

Jennifer Cox, "The Intubation Choir," *Room* 46.3

Nancy Jo Cullen, "Rogue," *EVENT* 52.1

Josie Di Sciascio-Andrews, "Octarine," *Poetry Pause* April 4, 2023

Farah Ghafoor, "Birthday Poem," *Canthius* 11

Bianca Giglio, "Tender," *yolk* 3.2

Patrick Grace, "The Calling," *The Malahat Review* 221

Jasmine Gui, "Resurgent Artefacts," *Vallum* 20.1

Warren Heiti, "House," *The Malahat Review* 224

Overcomer Ibiteye, "Home Is Here," *Qwerty* 46

Ayesha Jafar, "Pressure Cooker," *Room* 46.1

Meghan Kemp-Gee, "More symmetry," *The Fiddlehead* 296

Stefanie Kirby, "Illumination," *Qwerty* 46

EJ Kneifel, "Silly Fragile," *Grain* Fiftieth Anniversary Summer 2023

Grace Kwan, "Every Day on the 14 Down Hastings," *Room* 46.3

T. Liem, "Most Did Not Ask," *The Ampersand Review* 3

Annick MacAskill, "Praying for Rain," *yolk* 3.2

Tanis MacDonald, "Filing Meadowlarks," *Grain* 50.2

Murray Mann, "Ungulate Earth," EVENT 51.3

Suzette Mayr, "Maggot Love Poem," *Canadian Literature* 252

Vanessa McCuaig, "My Birthmark," *Prairie Fire* 44.1

Britt McGillivray, "I Want To Tell You," *Canthius* 11

rob mclennan, "Derecho," *The Peter F. Yacht Club* 31

Abby Nixon, "The Woman, the Grocer, and the Boy," *Prairie Fire* 44.1

John Pass, "Catch," *Grain* 51.1

Cale Plett, "Curtain," *Plenitude Magazine* April 15, 2023

Lisa Richter, "Winter Solstice," *Riddle Fence* 47

Matt Robinson, "Birch," *The Malahat Review* 224

Michael Russell, "Lorde of the Basement," *Qwerty* 47

Angeline Schellenberg, "First-Day Photo," *The Malahat Review* 223

Bren Simmers, "Overheard: Two Poems" *Contemporary Verse 2* 46.1

Cristalle Smith, "The Hierophant," *subTerrain* 94

Maya Somogyi, "Big Bang Never Ended," *The /tɛmz/ Review* 24

Kara Stanton, "New Moon in Taurus," *Room* 46.3

Neil Surkan, "Limits," *The Malahat Review* 223

Steffi Tad-y, "English Lessons in a Former Colony," *Room* 46.1

Maša Torbica, "Tautologies," *Canadian Literature* 253

Sarah Yi-Mei Tsiang, "The Obstetrician Names All the Dangers of Geriatric Pregnancy," *Prairie Fire* 44.1

Gabriel Waite, "Standards for Living," *Room* 46.2

Sarah Wolfson, "The Gravedigger," *Geist* 123

Ami Xherro, "March 1988," *Contemporary Verse 2* 45.3

MAGAZINES CONSULTED

Each year, the fifty best poems and the list of notable poems by Canadian poets are selected from more than sixty print and online journals published in the previous year. While direct submissions of individual poems are not accepted, we welcome review copies from print outlets and announcements of new issues from online publications. Please direct two copies of each print issue to Best Canadian Poetry c/o Biblioasis, 1686 Ottawa St., Ste 100, Windsor, ON N8Y 1R1, or email us at bestcanadianpoetry@biblioasis.com.

The Adroit Journal (theadroitjournal.org)

The Ampersand Review (theampersandreview.ca). Sheridan College, Hazel McCallion Campus, Room B220, 4180 Duke of York Blvd., Mississauga, ON L5B 0G5

The Antigonish Review (antigonishreview.com). PO Box 5000, Antigonish, NS, B2G 2W5

Arc Poetry Magazine (arcpoetry.ca). PO Box 269, Stn B, Ottawa, ON, K1P 6C4

Brick, A Literary Journal (brickmag.com). PO Box 609, Stn. P, Toronto, ON, M5S 2Y4

Bywords (bywords.ca)

Canadian Broadcasting Corporation, CBC Poetry Prize
finalists (cbc.ca)

Canadian Literature (canlit.ca). University of British
Columbia, Mary Bollert Hall, Room 111, 6253 NW Marine
Drive, Vancouver, BC, V6T 1Z1

Canthius (canthius.com)

The Capilano Review (thecapilanoreview.com). 210-111 West
Hastings St., Vancouver, BC, V6B 1H4

Carousel (carouselmagazine.ca). UC 274, University of Guelph,
Guelph, ON, N1G 2W1

carte blanche (carteblanchemagazine.com)

Columba Poetry (columbapoetry.com)

Contemporary Verse 2 (*CV2*) (contemporaryverse2.ca). 502–
100 Arthur St., Winnipeg, MB, R3B 1H3

Dalhousie Review (ojs.library.dal.ca/dalhousiereview).
Dalhousie University, Halifax, NS, B3H 4R2

EVENT (eventmagazine.ca). PO Box 2503, New Westminster,
BC, V3L 5B2

The Ex-Puritan (ex-puritan.ca)

Exile Quarterly (exilequarterly.com). Exile/Excelsior
Publishing Inc., 170 Wellington St. W., PO Box 308, Mount
Forest, ON, N0G 2L0

Feathertale (feathertale.com). PO Box 5023, Ottawa, ON, K2C 3H3

The Fiddlehead (thefiddlehead.ca). Campus House, University of New Brunswick, 11 Garland Ct., PO Box 4400, Fredericton, NB, E3B 5A3

filling Station (fillingstation.ca). PO Box 22135, Bankers Hall, Calgary, AB, T2P 4J5

FreeFall (freefallmagazine.ca). 250 Maunsell Close, NE Calgary, AB, T2E 7C2

Funicular Magazine (funicularmagazine.com)

Geist (geist.com). Suite 210, 111 W. Hastings St., Vancouver, BC, V6B 1H4

Grain (grainmagazine.ca). Saskatchewan Writers' Guild, Suite 100, 1150 8th Ave, Regina, SK, S4P 3R9

Granta (granta.com)

HA&L (*Hamilton Arts & Letters*) (halmagazine.wordpress.com)

Juniper (juniperpoetry.com)

The Leaf (brucedalepress.ca). PO Box 2259, Port Elgin, ON, N0H 2C0

Literary Review of Canada (reviewcanada.ca). Massey College, 4 Devonshire Place, Toronto, ON, M5S 2E1

long con magazine (longconmag.com)

Maisonneuve (maisonneuve.org). 1051 boul. Decarie, PO Box 53527, Saint Laurent, QC, H4L 5J9

The Malahat Review (malahatreview.ca). University of Victoria, PO Box 1700, Stn. CSC, Victoria, BC, V8W 2Y2

The Nashwaak Review (stu.ca/english/the-nashwaak-review). St. Thomas University, Fredericton, NB, E3B 5G3

The New Quarterly (tnq.ca). St. Jerome's University, 290 Westmount Rd. N., Waterloo, ON, N2L 3G3

The New Yorker (newyorker.com) 1 World Trade Center, New York, NY, 10007, USA

The Newfoundland Quarterly (nqonline.ca). Memorial University of Newfoundland, Signal Hill Campus, 100 Signal Hill Rd., St. John's, NL, A1C 5S7

Open Minds Quarterly (openmindsquarterly.com)

Parentheses (parenthesesjournal.com)

Peach (peachmgzn.com)

Periodicities (periodicityjournal.blogspot.com).

The Peter F. Yacht Club (abovegroundpress.blogspot.com)

Plenitude Magazine (plenitudemagazine.ca)

Poetry Pause (poets.ca/poetrypause)

The Polyglot (thepolyglotmagazine.com)

Prairie Fire (prairiefire.ca). 423–100 Arthur St., Winnipeg, MB, R3B 1H3

PRISM international (prismmagazine.ca). Creative Writing Program, University of British Columbia, Buchanan Room E462, 1866 Main Mall, Vancouver, BC, V6T 1Z1

Queen's Quarterly (queensu.ca/quarterly). Rm 215 Stauffer Library, Queen's University, 101 Union St., Kingston, ON, K7L 2N9

Qwerty (qwertyunb.com). University of New Brunswick Department of English, P.O. Box 4400, 19 Macaulay Lane, Fredericton, NB, E3B 5A3

Red Alder Review (redalderreview.wordpress.com)

Ricepaper Magazine (ricepapermagazine.ca). PO Box 74174, Centre Point Mall PO, Vancouver, BC, V5T 4E7

Riddle Fence (riddlefence.com)

Room (roommagazine.com). PO Box 46160, Stn. D, Vancouver, BC, V6J 5G5

Rust & Moth (rustandmoth.com)

subTerrain (subterrain.ca). PO Box 3008, MPO, Vancouver, BC, V6B 3X5

Talking About Strawberries (talkingaboutstrawberries.blogspot.com)

The /tƐmz/ Review (thetemzreview.com)

This Magazine (this.org). 417–401 Richmond St. W., Toronto, ON, M5V 3A8

Touch the Donkey (touchthedonkey.blogspot.com)

Train: a poetry journal (trainpoetryjournal.blogspot.com).

The Typescript (thetypescript.com)

untethered (alwaysuntethered.com)

Vallum (vallummag.com). 5038 Sherbrooke W., PO Box 23077, CP Vendome, Montreal, QC, H4A 1T0

The Walrus (walrusmagazine.com). 411 Richmond St. E., Suite B15, Toronto, ON, M5A 3S5

West End Phoenix (westendphoenix.com). The Gladstone Hotel, 1214 Queen St. W., Toronto, ON, M6J 1J6

Wildness (readwildness.com)

The Windsor Review (ojs.uwindsor.ca/index.php/windsor_review). Department of English, University of Windsor, 401 Sunset Ave., Windsor, ON N9B 3P4

yolk (yolkliterary.ca)

INDEX TO POETS

Adams, Hollie, 39

Amabile, George, 31

Bedford, Erin, 47

Belcourt, Billy-Ray, 25

Bickersteth, Bertrand, 95

Blair, Elisabeth, 64

Bloom, Ronna, 122

Braid-Fernandez, Alison, 79

Bringhurst, Robert, 74

Cann, Emily, 49

Carson, Anne, 51

Cross-Blanchard, Molly, 59

Crozier, Lorna, 35

Czaga, Kayla, 101

Ekoko-Kay, Evelyna, 89

Genevieve, Kate, 121

Gillis, Susan, 29

Goyette, Sue, 108

Graham, Catherine, 72

Heavyshield, Henry, 82

Hill, Gerald, 112

Hollenberg, Alexander, 93

Johnson, Kim June, 67

Joseph, Eve, 107

Lau, Evelyn, 80

Lee, Y. S., 58

Lockhart, D. A., 65

Malik, Fareh, 97

Martin, David, 111

Martinello, Domenica, 70

McFadzean, Cassidy, 105

McGrath, Carmelita, 118

Moure, Erín, 106

Oloruntoba, Tolu, 113

Owen, Catherine, 37

Peacock, Molly, 61

Pearson, Miranda, 27

Peters, Pauline, 63

Proctor, Amanda, 68

Quinn, Shannon, 38

Ruffo, Armand Garnet, 99

Simpson, Anne, 54

Smart, Carolyn, 57
Solie, Karen, 45
St. Denis, Catherine, 42
Torrey, Owen, 33

Trussler, Michael, 36
Truuvert, Sara, 123
Winger, Rob, 87
Yoo, Jaeyun, 92

ACKNOWLEDGEMENTS

"According to the CBC, Indigenous Peoples Are Demonstrably More Vulnerable to Illness and Disease, Live 15 Years Less Than Other Canadians" first appeared in *Arc Poetry Magazine* copyright © Billy-Ray Belcourt. Reprinted with permission of the author.

"Bridestones" first appeared in *Grain* copyright © Miranda Pearson. Reprinted from *Bridestones* by Miranda Pearson (McGill–Queens University Press, 2024) with permission of the author and publisher.

"Come In, Come In" first appeared in *The Fiddlehead* copyright © Susan Gillis. Reprinted with permission of the author.

"Coming of age on my 84th birthday" first appeared in *Poetry Pause* copyright © George Amabile. Reprinted with permission of the author.

"CV" first appeared in *The Malahat Review* copyright © Owen Torrey. Reprinted with permission of the author.

"December's End" first appeared in *Riddle Fence* copyright © Lorna Crozier. Appeared as "The First Night" from *After That:*

"Funny You Should Ask" was first published in *The New Yorker*. Reprinted by permission of Anne Carson and Aragi Inc. All rights reserved.

"The Golden Boat" first appeared in *The Fiddlehead* copyright © Anne Simpson. Reprinted with permission of the author.

"Grip" first appeared in *Grain* copyright © Carolyn Smart. Reprinted with permission of the author.

"He/him" first appeared in *Grain* copyright © Y. S. Lee. Reprinted with permission of the author.

"Here's the thing" first appeared in *Geist* copyright © Molly Cross-Blanchard. Reprinted with permission of the author.

"Honey Crisp" first appeared in *The Walrus*. From *The Widow's Crayon Box* by Molly Peacock. Copyright © 2024 by Molly Peacock. Used by permission of W. W. Norton & Company, Inc.

"Housebreaking" first appeared in *The Malahat Review* copyright © Pauline Peters. Reprinted with permission of the author.

"a hunt's surviving duck" first appeared in *Columba Poetry* copyright © Elisabeth Blair. Reprinted with permission of the author.

"Hussain Recites Ginsberg While Driving Down Kedzie" first appeared in EVENT copyright © D. A. Lockhart. Reprinted with permission of the author.

"I Don't Know What to Do about the World" first appeared in *The New Quarterly* copyright © Kim June Johnson. Reprinted with permission of the author.

"Orchids" first appeared in *Contemporary Verse 2* copyright ©
Jaeyun Yoo. Reprinted with permission of the author.

"origin story, with crow" first appeared in *Contemporary Verse
2* copyright © Alexander Hollenberg. Reprinted with
permission of the author.

"A Poem about Blackboy's Horse" first appeared in *The
Fiddlehead* copyright © Bertrand Bickersteth. Reprinted with
permission of the author.

"Praise Us, for We Are Dead" first appeared in *The Ex-Puritan*
copyright © Fareh Malik. Reprinted with permission of the
author.

"Resting II" first appeared in *Arc Poetry Magazine* copyright ©
Armand Garnet Ruffo. Reprinted from *The Dialogues* by
Armand Garnet Ruffo (Wolsak & Wynn, 2024) with
permission of the author and publisher.

"Safe Despair" first appeared in *The Malahat Review*. From
Midway copyright © 2024 by Kayla Czaga. Reproduced with
permission from House of Anansi Press, Toronto. www.
houseofanansi.com.

"Storm King" first appeared in *long con magazine*. From *Crying
Dress* copyright © 2024 by Cassidy McFadzean. Reproduced
with permission from House of Anansi Press, Toronto. www.
houseofanansi.com.

"The Straying of All Translation: A Phrase Archive" first
appeared in *The Polyglot* copyright © Erín Moure. Reprinted
with permission of the author.

EDITORS' BIOGRAPHIES

AISLINN HUNTER is an award-winning poet and novelist living on the unceded and ancestral lands of the Musqueam, Squamish and Tsleil-Waututh peoples. Her most recent book of poetry is *Linger, Still* (Gaspereau Press), winner of the Fred Cogswell Award for Excellence in Poetry.

ANITA LAHEY's latest poetry collection is *While Supplies Last* (Véhicule Press, 2023). She's also co-author, with Pauline Conley, of the 2023 graphic novel-in-verse *Fire Monster* (Palimpsest Press). Her 2020 memoir, *The Last Goldfish: a True Tale of Friendship* (Biblioasis), was an Ottawa Book Award finalist. Anita has worked with *Best Canadian Poetry* since 2014, and has served as series editor since 2018. She lives in Ottawa.